# No Dribbling the Squid

# No
# Dribbling
# the Squid

Octopush, Shin Kicking,
Elephant Polo, and
Other Oddball Sports

Michael J. Rosen

with Ben Kassoy

**Andrews McMeel**
**Publishing, LLC**
Kansas City • Sydney • London

09 10 11 12 13 CHO 10 9 8 7 6 5 4 3 2 1

ISBN-13: 978-0-7407-8120-9
ISBN-10: 0-7407-8120-0

Library of Congress Control Number: 2009923914

www.andrewsmcmeel.com

Book design by Holly Camerlinck
Cover photo by Grégory Piazzola

# contents

*in which we offer a roster of sports with annotations as needed; a complete list of all the sports mentioned in the book can be found on page 223.*

*That sweet adrenaline rush that comes from rushing around like a crazy person.*
*Competitions for people who wonder if they're faster than others at doing things that others aren't even eager to do slowly.*

## three: Recess Gone Wild . . . . . . . . . . . . . . . . . . . .55

*Childhood games now available in grown-up and overgrown sizes.*

## four: Mix-and-Match Sports . . . . . . . . . . . . . . . .87

*Did someone just pull random equipment from the phys ed closet and call it a new sport? Rebus games!*

# introduction

If you're like many of the enthusiasts who have pioneered, or at least pursued, the wildest and most wayward athletic competitions, *and* if you're still looking for the coolest, hottest, swiftest, toughest new rush, this is the collection for you. Here are umpteen ways to risk life and limb. That said, we must admit, right at the outset, that we set aside hundreds of other extreme, eccentric, and excellent but unfamiliar sports, each of which might enjoy its own volume one day—and more power to it!

- most of the motorized sports
- most events involving blades, boards, skis, kites, or camouflage
- nearly all of the numbingly numerous forms of wrestling and martial arts

Preferring quirkiness to completeness, we also overlooked competitions that left us wondering, well, "Huh?" These included:

- the Town Crier shout-offs, where the athletics consist of strong vocal cords and the breath control to recite announcements in a boisterous and authoritative manner

- Berlin's annual Stiletto Race, involving a hundred *Glamour* subscribers who run in high heels along a cordoned-off city street
- the Chinchilla Melon Festival, in which competitors smash as many watermelons with their foreheads in a minute as they can (John Allwood holds the current record of forty melons)

Still other "sports" seemed to require the use of quotes around the word "sports," which is not a good sign. They sounded more like a one-time tourist outing, such as:

- hanging from a harness and a parachute/kite while being towed by a speedboat as your fellow vacationers shoot MPEGs to post on YouTube
- pillow fighting in an actual league, rather than at a slumber party
- rolling down a hill *inside* a human-size plastic ball known as a Zorb, or "running" on the water inside a similarly sized bubble

We also declined sports involving animals who weren't likely to be enjoying themselves quite as much as the humans. For instance:

- racing cows and other barnyard animals
- riders on the backs of galloping ostriches
- competing in Buzhashi, where players, mounted on horses, whack a goat's head across the playing field

You are welcome to call us humaniacs.

Not that we had hard and fast rules, or that we wouldn't have broken them if we had them.

We set out to unearth Earth's most whacky and wanton pastimes, where creativity and athletic competition come together like two mud wrestlers with a satisfying and viscous *thwack*. We seined. We dredged. We poked a flashlight— with fresh batteries, no less—into every locker- and chat room we could find. We ransacked cabanas, college libraries, camp scrapbooks, and fraternity archives. And, like anthropologists raiding tombs, or maybe naturalists snatching specimens from the wild, we've made an exhibit! Here are those sporting events with an unqualified capacity to surprise, thrill, shock, tax the body, and send you asking, "Why in the world would anyone ever want to . . . ?"

Over and over, we knew there were readers who would want to know, right off, which are the most reckless sports? Which are the most expensive? Where can I find the ones most likely to include what we've come to know as "wardrobe failures"?

And so we wrestled (both toe- and Bavarian-finger-style—see page 83) about how to present the hundred or so sports gathered under the umbrella of oddball sports we picked one day that it was raining really, really hard.

We considered classifying sports by degree of experience needed. For instance, in these three chapters: (1) Try this at home, (2) try this at *someone else's* home, and (3) *let someone else* try this first at his or her home.

We tried a table of contents based on country of origin, but, oddly, we found nice chapters on Finland, Japan, the United Kingdom (and New Zealand and Australia), but lots of other countries were left feeling slighted and pouty.

We tried the sort of icons that travel brochures and dog-breed guides use to suggest "water-friendly" or "not good for children" or "only for the experienced." Here are a few we came up with:

= **requires pregame inebriation:** Tower Jumping, Shin Kicking, Shrovetide Football, Wine Battle, *Calcio Storico*

= **postgame anesthesia required:** Tower Jumping, Shin Kicking, Shrovetide Football, Wine Battle, *Calcio Storico*, Splashdiving, Rock, Paper, Scissors, Outhouse Racing, Cyclocross, BASE Jumping

= **requires expensive equipment** that you're likely to end up putting on eBay: Swooping, Cyclocross, Ice Racing

= you can **make your own home version of the game** for less than the price of a souvenir program: Bog Snorkeling, Broomball,

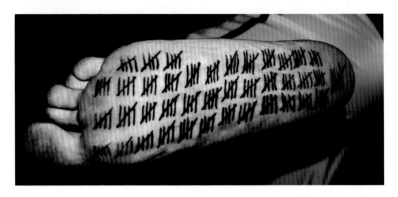

Cheese Rolling, Extreme Ironing, Hurling Events, Joggling, Mudslinging Festival, Naked Men Festival, Retro Running, Retro Cycling, Shovel Racing, Extreme Soccers, Speed Cubing, Sport Stacking, Spitting Contests, Finger- and Toe Wrestling

= **choking hazard:** Spitting Contests, Kabaddi, Wine Battle, Extreme Cold-Water Swimming, Octopush, Barefooting, Bog Snorkeling

= **choking hazard:** *Calcio Storico*, Shrovetide Football, Mudslinging Festival, Naked Men Festival

Then we realized that almost all of the sports covered here involve inebriation, anesthesia, unusual equipment, and choking hazards—and often all of those things together.

We finally decided to just offer you here eight convenient chapters organized by some common nuttiness. That said, you may dip in anywhere—each entry is complete unto itself—or read the book straight through in one sitting as if speed reading were your kind of athletic race.

# "There's Nothing to Fear But the Sport Itself" Guide

Assuming you have a healthy appreciation of danger in its various guises, as well as a working knowledge of your own physical and psychological limitations, this list of phobias may be useful as you consider your next idyllic sport.

**Acrophobia** (fear of heights): BASE Jumping, Swooping, Sky Surfing, Bossaball, Extreme Ironing, Fierljeppen, Kiiking, Elephant Polo, Splashdiving, Tower Jumping

**Claustrophobia** (fear of tight places): *Calcio Storico*, Extreme Ironing, Mudslinging Festival, Naked Men Festival, Outhouse Racing, Sauna Competition, *La Tomatina*, Orange Battle, Wine Battle

**Emetophobia** (fear of vomiting): Spitting Contests, Haggis Hurling, Outhouse Racing, Kiiking, Bog Snorkeling

**Amaxophobia** (fear of riding in vehicles): Sky Surfing, Swooping, Cyclocross, Ice Racing, Ice Yachting, Mower Racing, Canoe Polo, Retro Cycling, Shovel Racing, Unicycle Events

**Atelophobia** (fear of falling short, as in imperfection): Baby Jumping, Chess Boxing, Speed Cubing, Sport Stacking, Fierljeppen, Wife-Carrying Race

**Myxophobia** (fear of slime): Bog Snorkeling, Bog Cycling, Swooping, Fierljeppen

**Cheimaphobia** (fear of cold): Extreme Cold-Water Swimming, Naked Men Festival, Mudslinging Festival, Ice Racing, *Yukigassen*, Extreme Ironing, Ice Yachting, Snow Soccer, Shovel Racing

**Cymophobia** (fear of waves): Skimboarding, Barefooting, Octopush, Canoe Polo

**Gymnophobia** (fear of nudity): Naked Men Festival, Mudslinging Festival, Outhouse Racing

**Tachophobia** (fear of speed): Barefooting, Swooping, BASE Jumping, Sky Surfing, Ice Racing, Ice Yachting, Shovel Racing

# one

## The Thrill of the Spill

Call them thrill seekers, adrenaline junkies, fringe freaks, daredevils, double-dare devils, eXercise eXtremists, utter jackasses, or a name of your choosing—some athletes' chosen sport seems to be an insatiable quest for that Next Big Rush. The rest of us, those of us content with that Last Little Rush, can only imagine it:

"So . . . is it sort of like how, first thing when I wake up, I just crave a cup of coffee?"

Yeah, right. Your little jolt of java is nothing compared to pure adrenaline. That's the body's triple espresso with six sugars! So while these folks are leaping off precipices, careening on sleds down interstates, or skiing skiless while facing backward behind a speeding powerboat, the rest of us can only sigh and say, "I'm glad your mother isn't here to witness this. And you were such a sweet baby, even with the colic."

For these endorphin addicts, the standard means of risking life and limb are pseudonyms for satisfaction, mere stand-ins for "what's the big deal?" In this chapter, we stand at some of the new boundaries they've crossed, giddily leaning over to snap a few camera-phone pix to show friends back home that we were right there! Right there where the Next Big Thing (We'd Never Dream of Doing) is taking place.

**"If a blister or cut opens on the bottom of an athlete's foot, glue it shut now to finish skiing and deal with the stitches later."*

—USA Water Ski

Walking barefoot on the beach provides that ineffable carefree feeling. Removing your shoes before entering a mosque shows respect. Ditching your boots before entering someone's home that's decorated with expensive white Berber carpeting suggests that you like fussy friends who don't own dogs. But to water-ski without skis can only prove how much better you think you are than everyone else on land and sea. (*Go ahead, do it on one foot! Pull a 360! Prove the point!*)

Barefoot skiing, self-satisfyingly known simply as barefooting, got its feet wet in Florida in the '40s and '50s, a full decade before

* From the American Barefoot Club official Web site. Indeed, a tube of superglue is the only item in the barefoot skier's "equipment" kit.

Australia began holding national competitions. The first world championships were held in 1978—the very year Volkswagen stopped manufacturing Beetles and the first cell phones were introduced. Uncanny!

Those in the mood to kick off their shoes—skis, really—compete in three events:

**slalom:** Skiers cross in and out of the wake as many times as possible, on one foot or two, skiing backward or forward.

**jump:** Skiers fly off an 18-inch ramp as the speedboat is splashing across the current at 40 miles per hour.

**tricks:** Skiers perform two fifteen-second passes and pull off as many daring maneuvers as possible (e.g., holding the rope in the teeth, facing backward, somersaulting).

The American Barefoot Club and World Barefoot Council sanction the events and log in official records such as David Small's 89-foot, 11-inch jump in 2004. If an average blue whale had surfaced to watch the goofiness, David would have sailed its entire length . . . while the whale would have thought to itself, "So *this* is how far we've come in mammalian evolution? At least *dolphins* are intelligent."

Barefooting might look simple, but getting up is very difficult, since feet don't glide on the water's surface as easily as skis, unless your feet are 66 inches by 6 inches—in other words, the exact size of a ski or a Cirque du Soleil contortionist. That said, faster boat speeds are

required for an athlete to plane on two bare feet. A skier holds onto the rope leaning forward and is pulled onto his stomach as the boat begins to move. As the boat accelerates, the skier begins to plane on the water and can rotate from his stomach onto his back and, from there, stand up. Once one has mastered the "tumble-up" start, the trick is then to avoid the more painful "tumble down" back onto the water.

Get a (bare)foot in the door at www.barefoot.org.

## Lose the Shoes!

With the exemption of some gymnastic, martial art, and aquatic competitions, shouldn't other sports rise to the challenge of going barefoot? When will special events evolve for shoeless figure skating, mountain climbing, flamenco dancing, cycling, snowboarding, horse racing (come on! It's already done bareback!), or weightlifting? It's not as if a fear of splinters, bee stings, or stepping in manure is justifiable in every sport.

Lest you think this is the most peculiar form of skiing, competitors at Australia's Chinchilla Melon Festival attempt to ski for as long as possible with one foot wedged inside each of two enormous watermelons.

# "Swooping is like combining NASCAR with aviation."

—Pro Swooping Tour Web site

## Swooping

When one is high in the air, the idea is normally to do what you went all the way up there to do—dunk your basketball; fly to Oslo for the a-ha reunion concert; reach the tin of almond bark hidden in the top cupboard so you won't eat it all in one sitting—and get back on the ground as quickly as possible. But not in the sport of swooping.

Also known as canopy piloting, swooping has competitors called pilots who jump from a plane (upon learning there was no a-ha concert after all?), release a small "performance" parachute, and navigate upon or just above the surface of a body of water at a speed of 90 miles per hour. If executed incorrectly, swooping becomes indistinguishable from the '60s B-movie *Voyage to the Bottom of the Sea*.

*Real* pilots fly 747s, cut ahead in security lines, and get to have free cocktails with flight attendants. *Swooping* pilots compete in three types of competitions:

In the **speed event,** pilots must finish a straightaway as quickly as possible, never touching the water's surface, but swooping just above it.

In the **distance event,** pilots fly as far as possible over the water's surface without making the slightest contact.

The **accuracy event** has pilots negotiate a series of gates above the water and land within a specific zone at the course's end.

As if the sport weren't hard-core enough, giving swooping a **freestyle competition** is like giving a rapper more ego or an audiophile another one of those velvet album cleaners. Points are based on approach, time on the water, execution of acrobatic and creative maneuvers, and landing. Pilots on the Pro Swooping Tour execute a series of spins, jumps, and grabs, often backward, one-footed, or on their knees, in tricks that are named after superheroes—Ghost Rider, Superman, and Lazy Boy.

Swooping is also practiced on land and in the mountains, where it's known as blade running and often takes place on ski slopes, where competitors launch themselves from either mountaintops or planes, in order to weave among vertical flags known as airblades.

You can have almost as much fun at home! Make your own

performance 'chute out of a handkerchief, tie it to an action figure, and toss it out a second-floor window. This version is also a lot safer.

Looking for more spectator-friendly skydiving? Everything happens at ground level at www.proswoopingtour.tv.

## BASE Jumping

**"If there is a God, he must look down and say, 'Look, the thing I made them the most afraid of, they went and turned into a friggin' sport.'"**
—BASE jumper Nick DiGiovanni

Yes, BASE is an acronym, which makes you think it's just another boring corporation. But is boring ever delivered at a speed of 100 miles per hour? No, BASE stands for Building, Antennae, Spans, Earth—all "things you can jump off of."

The concept and acronym were coined in 1978 by filmmaker Carl Boenish after he jumped off the world's largest granite block, El Capitan (3,000 feet) at California's Yosemite National Park. Since then, despite legality issues and the extreme dangers of the sport (more than 123 fatalities occurred between 1981 and 2008, including Boenish himself in 1984), jumpers have covered the Eiffel Tower, Seattle's Space Needle, antennas all over the world, and a Guinness World Record–breaking 21,667-foot jump from a peak in India.

For one day in October every year, city officials in Fayetteville, West Virginia, turn a blind eye to Bridge Day, during which jumpers conquer the second highest bridge in the United States, which overlooks the New River Gorge. For six hours, BASE jumping from the bridge is "legal," as 200,000 spectators watch 450 jumpers plummet 876 feet down into the gorge below.

To receive a BASE number, an athlete must jump at least once in each category or letter of the acronym. BASE-1 was awarded to Phil Smith in 1981. Matt Moilanen received the one thousandth BASE

number in 2005, finally answering the question, "If your best friend jumped off a cliff (or bridge or building or antenna), would you do it too?"

Has your answer always been yes? Check out www.blincmagazine.com.

## Skysurfing

**"Not even NASA astronauts get to play in four dimensions."**
—Official free fallers at the Dropzone Web site

About thirty years ago, thanks to the country that brought the sporting universe croquet, pool, petanque, pari-mutuel track betting, automobile racing, Greco-Roman wrestling (yes, the French named the sport in honor of those buff boys painted on those urns), and one long-ass bike race, some skydivers began skysurfing, in which jumpers stand on a board and perform a series of spins, somersaults, and other tricks during a plummet to Earth.

A Reebok commercial featuring French skysurfers brought the sport to America in 1991. It was demonstrated at the 1994 Lilleham-mer Olympics. The X Games featured skysurfing from 1995 to 2000. All this broadened sky-surfing's appeal, if "broad" can refer to the dubious minions of folks clamoring to exit an airplane on a surfboard.

Today, the International Parachuting Commission hosts the Sky-surfing World Championships, which awards points based on video camera footage. According to the skydiving info center, www.dropzone.com, in this two-person team sport "the cameraflyer records the performance [of the skysurfer] with a helmet-mounted camcorder but also contributes to the performance interactively—and the team's overall score—through his or her own creative and athletic skills." Imagine if other athletes had personal videographers: There'd be paparazzi stealing signs in every baseball dugout, no use for line judges at tennis matches, and technologically sanctioned "peeking" at other players' hands during the World Series of Poker.

Skysurfing lives in tetraspace. (Steady now . . . you can wrap your head around this bit of physics.) If Hugh Grant is one-dimensional; Ms. Pac-Man, two-dimensional; and friends (in person, not on the Internet), three-dimensional; then four is the magic number for skysurfing. Out in tetraspace, skysurfing uniquely provides athletes the power to maneuver move up/down, left/right, and forward/backward, *and* to control their relative speed, which counts as a fourth dimension if you enjoy science, science fiction, or psychotropic mushrooms.

Long for the chance to shout "Gnarly!" from 10,000 feet? See www.skysurfer.com.

**Pull your own weight . . . or let an animal do it for you**

Humans are in a constant struggle to decide what matters more: our relationship with dogs and horses, those lovable companions, those "four-legged members of the family"; or our need to get somewhere faster than our own two feet can carry us.

Factor in some snow and an additional pair of skis (oh, and the accompanying $900 seasonal membership and the inevitable snot that congeals over much of your face), and your decision morphs into a true dilemma. One answer is skijøring, where we can simply attach ourselves to Sparky, Max, or Mr. Bo Jingles, and ski behind them.

## Not Just Along for the Ride

Dogs, unlike horses, cannot be ridden around a corral.

Horses, unlike dogs, cannot catch a Frisbee or sleep next to you on your new pillow-top mattress.

Neither seem to survive in movies where they are the best friend of the troubled juvenile protagonist.

Both are found in Budweiser commercials and—luckily for us—in the two most popular forms of skijøring. (Also popular, especially with those who have neither large dogs nor abiding horses: skijøring behind snowmobiles or other motorized vehicles.) Here is a brief comparison of the two beastly versions of the sport.

| What's on your mind? | Equine | Canine |
|---|---|---|
| So what's the basic idea here? | A rope is attached to a horse's saddle, which pulls you, the skier, down a straightaway course. | About the same, but you ski cross-country style. Doggie sweaters are strictly prohibited. |
| What composes a team? | Two people (one rider, one skier); one horse | One person; one, two, or three dogs |
| Is there a governing body, or can I call the shots? | The North American Ski Joring Association. Popular competition spots include Minneapolis and Quebec. You can bet that Dubai will feature skijøring before Acapulco. | After a prolonged mutt-iny, the International Federation of Sleddog Sports is now run solely by the canines themselves, making the organization entirely FDBD (For Dogs, By Dogs). |

| What's on your mind? | Equine | Canine |
| --- | --- | --- |
| How long's the course? | It's typically between 850 and 1,000 feet. (For comparison, the Kentucky Derby is 10 furlongs.) (Okay, we'll look it up for you: 10 furlongs equals 6,600 feet.) | A **sprint** is 3–10 miles. An **endurance** race is 20–50 miles, a great workout for both humans and canines who spend most nights tethered to the couch watching reruns, munching on/beggin' for cheddar popcorn. |
| How long of a rope do I need to hook up to the horse or dog? | A rope that's 33 feet. For those keen on a less intense experience, a rope between 849 and 999 feet will do. | Depending on the number of dogs, a rope between 8 and 12 feet is standard. |
| If the animals are providing all the power, am I just along for the ride? | In a **shooting event**, you weave in and out of gates on the course, shooting a series of balloons—ruining some poor kid's birthday party—as you pass. In a **rings event**, you slalom between cones and land two to three jumps (3–6 feet high), while collecting rings hung from an apparatus along the course. | For a **distance race**, the course can be 20 miles or as long as 320 miles—about the distance of a road trip from Chicago to Des Moines. Skijorers prepare with a "working knowledge of winter survival" and additional supplies, including a map and a wife to say, "For chrissake, let's just stop and ask someone for directions!" |

| What's on your mind? | Equine | Canine |
| --- | --- | --- |
| How fast will I be going, because, you know, it's all about the adrenaline? | Up to 40 miles per hour. That's fast enough for a $160.80 speeding ticket in Minneapolis if you're in a residential area. | Up to 30 miles per hour, slow enough to avoid a ticket—unless you're in Minneapolis, which is Minnesota's worst speed trap, according to *USA Today*. |
| Which breeds are commonly hitched up? | Most any breed, except Clydesdales (Budweiser has exclusive rights on those) and centaurs. | Typically huskies, but any dog greater than 30 pounds will be in "canine ecstasy," according to the skiers. |
| How long has this silliness been going on? Er, I mean, when did something serious start sounding silly? | Skijøring began in Scandinavian countries hundreds of years ago as a means for long travel. It arrived in North America in the 1950s but only began to grow in popularity once skiers figured out how to make the "ø" symbol. | Although its country of origin is unclear, it is said that skijøring is a descendant of the Scandinavian *pulka,* in which riders, seated on what looks like half a canoe, scuttled around Lapland behind a team of reindeer. |

Right: When there's no snow in Australia, Rex and Darren Higgins (also pictured skijøring) go the dry-land sledding route. Also known as dog scootering, racers compete with two-wheeled scooters, or three- or four-wheeled chariots called rigs or gigs.

# Who Let the Dogs Out?

Just as in dog walking, where the canines often walk the humans, dog power is proving to be alternative energy with fewer negatives than wind towers or corn-based ethanol. In **bikejoring,** for example, dogs can take you for a spin around the neighborhood. In **dog scootering,** you can keep both feet onboard at all times. **Canicross,** where dogs take their owners on a cross-country run, has its own world championship. Once you start imagining what other things a dog or a horse might pull, it's easy to begin wondering . . . what other "species" might humans yet draft into drafting?

Domesticate your wildest sports ambitions at www.nasja.com (horses) and www.sleddogcentral.com (dogs).

## "Many are cold, but few are frozen."

—Central New York Ice Racing Association Inc.

Caption to come

Driving can be a real ordeal. Along with watching for tailgaters, impatient commuters passing on the right, SUVs towing swaying trailers, and deer in your headlights or on the side of the road, we are forced to deal with:

- dear old Grammie, who's in no special hurry to buy her grand-son tube socks at Kohl's
- the miniskirted, leggings-clad driver's ed grad Lisa OMGing her BFF Jill
- the motorcyclist imagining that his own personal lane exists between the baffles of the side-view mirrors in two lanes of stopped traffic
- the guy two lanes over whose stereo's bass is rattling *your* cup in its console holder

Now, put all of these menaces on what mothers describe as "It's a sheet of glass out there! You are *not* leaving the house!" and you reach a whole new iced plane of hazardousness, road rage, and car insurance.

## Motorcycles

*" . . . Known for speed, bumping and grinding action, and their lack of rules."*
—World Championship Ice Racing

If you're going to be obnoxiously loud, at least temper it with redeeming qualities. (This is general wisdom, not intended only for Fran Drescher and Bill O'Reilly.) Motorcycles, on the other hand, can take a straight-away at 80 miles per hour and a bend at 60—while on an ice hockey rink—and never lose a moment's sleep over decibel level. (Just FYI, 84 decibels is the maximum noise permitted in motorcycle ice racing, which is just above the sound of your vacuum cleaner and 26 decibels shy of a revved-up chain saw—neither of which, as it turns out, has any ice-racing potential.)

Steering one of these bikes on a frozen lake or speed skating oval ain't easy, but tire studs do help: They're ice-racing's equivalent of soccer cleats or baseball spikes. These screws or bolts attach to the tires and increase speed and traction, the latter being especially useful on turns where riders lean at an angle that puts the motorcycle literally inches from the track's surface. Think short-track speed skating, but with a 300-pound Yamaha as opposed to a thick-thighed South Korean in an Aquaman suit.

Since the first recorded race in Germany in 1925, motorcycles have been ice racing all over Europe, Canada, and the United States, most notably in competitions hosted by ICE. (Of course they had to have ICE for their acronym! It hardly matters that International Championship Events seems to apply to anything.)

The ICE tour features the same basic race with divisions for different vehicles:

**Manufacturers World Cup Bikes:** These lightweight and powerful bikes, created by major motorcycle companies such as Honda and Kawasaki, are like the marshmallow bits in the bowl of cereal that is ice racing.

**Big Dogs:** Also known as pit bikes, these miniature motorcycles are more likely to gnaw on your shoe than defend the yard against those damn kids who cut through the yard on their way to school.

**Unlimited Outlaw Quads:** Since 1985, ICE's four-wheel ATVs have received notoriety for their speed and bumper-car mentality.

**Ice-Breaker Amateur Quads:** Conversation with your therapist going nowhere? Bail on the banter! Come down from your seat in the bleachers, hop on one of these four-wheeled machines, and compete on the track against other spectators. Talk about breaking the ice with an actual ice breaker.

**XTreme Karts:** These are little round go-karts with a cockpit windshield just large enough to act as a protective cup.

Trade your bandanna and leather jacket for a motocross helmet and snowsuit at www.icespeedway.com.

## Automobiles

**"A full set of snow tires is recommended."**
—Michigan Ice Racing Association

The Adirondack Motor Enthusiast Club called automobile ice racing "the safest and most inexpensive form of road racing available today." Watching a five-year-old *vroom-vroom* miniature cars down a toy freeway, most parents would dispute this claim.

Nonetheless, automobile ice racing has gained recreational popularity in Canada and the northern United States, where the possibility of ice and roadways go together the way oil spills and waterways sort of go with the coastal states. The French, however, dominate this slippery sport, hosting and invariably winning the annual Trophée Andros Series, which reinforces the American feeling of inferiority, especially hearing the taunts of *"Mangez mon gel!"* (translation: "Eat my frost!") in that mellifluously pretentious tongue of theirs.

Without the strictures of an indoor "rink," cars can average 70 miles per hour during these outdoor races and often reach top speeds of over 100 miles per hour. Most makes and models of cars are appropriate for ice racing, except, of course, any car that someone wants to drive to work the next morning.

Winter blues get you red-hot? Check out www.icerace.com.

> " . . . For the love of . . . racing down a hill . . . we've had everything from rocket scientists . . . bums, drunks, stockbrokers, Microsoft programmers, and horse dentists doing this, but we all come together in peace and harmony."

—Street luger posting on www.street-luge.com

Taking something to the street can be quite interesting: community parades; neighbors sharing dishes at block parties; escaped zoo animals or convicts. Even the poor old English language, put out on the street, gets a whole lot of "fo' shizzle, my nizzle."

Street luge is no different: Long-haired, tatted-up, leather-suited playboys lying face-up on customized skateboards zoom up to 80 miles per hour, and not on an expertly engineered course as in the Olympics, but, rather, on your average time-for-the-daily-commute road. Potholes, soft shoulders, bacon (see page 25), bystanders—they're all part of the sport's standard thoroughfare.

Street luge is a descendant of "butt boarding" (or, to the over-protective parent, "tushy sledding") and has evolved from a pilot riding an elongated skateboard to a specifically designed board, equipped with a headrest, foot pegs, and a cup holder for a two-liter bottle of sugar-free *chutzpah*. Riders often access these reserves, as a Kevlar suit and motorcycle helmet don't change the fact that they maneuver tight turns by simply leaning a little to one side or the other and literally burn rubber—the soles of their shoes—to brake.

Debate on luge's origins continues to rage, particularly in California and Switzerland. (Oddly, credit for encouraging a person to consume half a pound of melted cheese at a single sitting didn't satisfy the Swiss ego.) All do concede, however, that the first organized street-luge event took place in Signal Hill, California. That 1978 race ended quickly with injuries to both competitors and spectators. After street luge's national debut at the inaugural X Games in 1995, and its appearance in ad campaigns from McDonald's and Mountain Dew, street luge looked to become the new face of fast food and attention deficit disorder.

Today, the International Gravity Sports Association (IGSA) holds a world championship, along with events in Canada, South Africa, and several European nations. And while the last six winners of the World

Cup Series have represented five countries, the undisputed champion every time—with the incredible speed of 9.8 m/s$^2$—is gravity itself.

Smart? Probably not. *Street* smart? Definitely.

Englishman Joel "The Gravity King" King once traveled 112.7 miles per hour on a luge he equipped with a jet pack. Want to try for lucky 113? Visit www.igsaworldcup.com.

## Street (Luge) Slang

Just a few bits of luging lingo to impress any friends who would even know (or care) what you're talking about.

**bacon:** a rough, uneven, or otherwise hazardous stretch of road.

**banana:** a rider whose luge frequently slips out from under him.

**chucking bale:** crashing into the hay bales—used as barriers along the track—with enough force to move them out of place.

**drop a hill:** to ride a luge course, preferably a closed one.

**flame:** when a street luge's wheels catch fire. (Another reason street luge kicks ice luge's ass.)

**flesh wing:** when a pilot extends an arm for balance during a difficult part of the course.

**puke a wheel:** losing a wheel as a result of flames or melting.

**rafting:** when a pilot is forced to regain speed by propelling himself with his hands after an unplanned stop or loss of momentum.

**road rash:** scrapes and skin burns after falling off a luge or after a collision.

**scrambled eggs:** a rough stretch of road, but to a lesser extent (and with less impact on your "good" cholesterol) than bacon.

**wad:** a multi-luge collision.

**wobbs:** the shaking or wobbling of the luge when reaching very high speeds.

---

### Downhill From Here

Not up for throwing caution to the wind? Consider these other downhill sports sanctioned by the International Gravity Sports Association.

**downhill skateboard:** Riders conquer steep hills with boards that are specifically engineered for more control as they reach speeds of up to 50 miles per hour.

**downhill inline:** Take those blades to the slopes at up to 75 miles per hour in a sport that, according to Inline Online, "only takes a small pebble or crack to toss you into a tree or car."

**gravity bike:** These smaller, modified bikes make pedaling obsolete when you're zooming at 90 miles per hour.

---

"I have 'hill hunter fever'—being preoccupied while driving and scouting new spots to ride."

—Street luger Kolby Parks

# two

## Misplaced Races

Four-time Indy 500 winner Rick Mears once said, "to finish first, you must first finish." Okay, so he knows something about racing. But if he knew anything about the competitions in this chapter, he might amend his advice to something like, "to finish first, you must first start."

Indeed, while he was breaking sound barriers over in Indiana, a few forward-thinking—or maybe just foggy-headed—folks forged ahead and founded events you've probably never even dreamed of winning, trials you can't imagine trying out, competitions you'd have been happy to approach with a simple, "No, *you* go first."

In this section, you'll see how (and why) these sporting enthusiasts decide to mow, shovel, or even stack plastic cups at the sound of the starting gun, while others elect to cross the finish lines of their respective races shoving garden tillers, sitting in outhouses, or mounted on bicycle handlebars.

"Slow and steady," contrary to the axiom, does *not* win any of these races. Depending on your choice of misplaced race, you might try "wed and not-too-weighty" as in Wife-Carrying Races, "breakneck and ballistic" as in Shovel Racing, or "nimble and nerdy" as in Speed Cubing.

And yet, sometimes even the best don't heed what's clearly sound advice. Said another Indy 500 winner, "I'm going to take it nice and easy. With my experience, I know you don't win a race on the first lap." Apparently Helio Castroneves never tried solving five 3x3 Rubik's Cubes in a minute, or zooming down a ski slope in the bucket of a coal shovel.

Usually it's the wife who drags the husband—out of bed to rake the leaves on a Sunday morning, to the mall to pick out new bedroom curtains and see the new Renée Zellweger chick flick, or to the hospital when her water breaks.

And yet, at the Wife-Carrying World Championships, held annually in Sonkajärvi, Finland, it's the husband who does the schlepping—the wife holds on for dear life—across a course that's over two and a half football fields in length and punctuated with sand, hurdles, water obstacles, and gravel pits.

And if you're not ready for commitment (or for the rest of that "in sickness and in health" crap), just grab any woman. As long as she's over seventeen (don't even *think* about going younger) and

108 pounds, your "wife" is legal. (Slimmer competitors must wear weighted rucksacks to bring them up to the minimum poundage.)

The race, which has been held since 1992, draws over forty couples and nearly eight thousand spectators. According to the Finnish Tourist Board, "The Wife Carrying creates a cheerful, bright and imaginative picture of Finland and we aim at using this image in marketing Finland." Indeed, the competition has nineteenth-century roots: It is said that a brigand of Vikings trained prospective members by forcing them to haul heavy rucksacks or livestock on their backs. The gang also had an affinity for stealing wives from neighboring villages (some say, to the delight of the neighboring husbands).

Despite its history, competitors constantly try out new techniques to improve their spousal swiftness. "It is of great importance to find a mutual rhythm," the organizers write. "If the wife on the man's back is

rocking out of time, the speed slows down." Practice, they say, is also essential: "It is possible to train . . . in the middle of the daily routines: In the bath, in the super market, in the playground, or in the body-building center."

Among the hauling techniques husbands employ are:

- traditional piggyback (her arms around his neck, her legs around his waist)
- the sack-of-potatoes carry (wife over one of his shoulders)
- fireman's carry (wife across both of his shoulders)
- "Estonian-style" carry (wife hanging upside down against his back, her legs wrapped around his shoulders, her arms clasped around his waist)

The last method is the easiest for returning the wife to her feet—the husband merely drops to his knees. (It's a familiar enough position, the one apologetic husbands assume after guys' nights out or when they forget to take the coupon caddy when going to get the frozen yogurt.)

One couple who employ the Estonian-style technique, are—*surprise*—Estonians Margo Uusorg and Birgit Ulricht, who managed to cross the "Finnish" line in a world-record time of 55.5 seconds.

And while Birgit's slight (prepadding) weight of 75 pounds helped them claim the title, it significantly cut down their winnings: The first place couple receives the equivalent of the wife's weight in beer. (The winners also receive a trophy and a bag of "wife-carrying products." Take a moment to imagine what those could possibly be.)

While competitions like this are becoming a global phenomenon—Australia, Hong Kong, and the United States also host events—each upholds the original Finnish rule: "All participants must have fun." Indeed, the last time carrying your wife proved this enjoyable was over the threshold on your wedding night.

Maine isn't so far, really. At the state's North American Wife Carrying Championships, www.sundayriver.com/Events/Main/FallFestival.html, winners receive the woman's weight in beer and five times her weight in cash. Or go global at www.sonkajarvi.fi/?deptid=15228.

### Other Partnering Plays

In the **sprint relay,** a man carries a woman, puts her down, and drinks a beer before the next man (the second of three) picks her up. The third man completes the 100-meter race in what appears to be a rather primitive and unsatisfying form of connubial bliss.

In the **marathon,** the husbands piggyback their wives and run as far as they can in six minutes. As the committee explains it: "The core of the race is made of a woman, a man, and their relationship. The wife carrying and eroticism have a lot in common. Intuitive understanding of the signals sent by the partner and becoming one with the partner are essential in both of them—sometimes also whipping."

"**Each outhouse must have material to wipe with.**"

—Mackinaw City Outhouse Race

With the advent of indoor plumbing, traditional outhouses suffered a tragic fate: They were mounted on skis and pushed down a hill.

In 1993, the people of Trenary, a town on Michigan's Upper Peninsula, decided to call that a sport and began hosting the annual Outhouse Classic. Trenarians continue to hold this event the last weekend in February, where teams of three—two pushers and one rider (that's right, they ride *there*)—construct outhouses, equip them with a mounted roll of toilet paper, and then race the boxes down a 500-foot course in front of thousands of potty-mouthed spectators.

Similar events now take place in Mackinaw City, Michigan; in Conocully, Washington; and as part of Alaska's Fur Rondy Festival. (Apparently, like dysentery, the sport is highly contagious.)

Trenary's Outhouse Classic awards competitors for winning the race, best presentation, most humorous, people's choice, best overall, and farthest traveled.

Feel free to make your own award categories for the photos here: *Most Immature? Punniest? Most Likely to Go to Pot?*

Feeling flush? Visit the Official Outhouses of America Tour: www.jldr.com/ohindex_ohracing.shtml.

**"More than words can, a backward motion of our bodies will provoke a fundamental questioning of our commonest attitudes and bring about the social change that the urgency and gravity of the problems of our day require."**

According to Professor Patrick Baronnet and his colleagues, this is why people participate in the sport of retro running (sometimes called backward running). Not simply to keep the sun out of their eyes, avoid taking a dust storm head on, or leave misleading footprints in the snow?

**"If we don't understand quickly that it's necessary to go backwards at all levels, then soon we will not be able to live on the earth."**

Aside from springing what these folks explain as an "extraordinary global evolution," retro runners also do it for the bounty of health benefits. Compared to forward running, retro running offers:

- better oxygenation (84 percent VO2 compared to 60 percent VO2)—unless you're a blood vessel, in which case you don't need to be reading this book, just trust us on this one
- a more intense workout of the quads (those are the quadriceps, the muscle group stretching from hip to knee—your thigh, basically—that works to extend your knee)
- less impact, meaning a gentler pounding on your feet, ankles, and knees
- better overall body flexibility (essentially, more willingness to go with the flow since you can't really see where you're going anyway)
- increased cardiovascular activity
- greater burning of calories—up to 33 percent more
- a greater interest in bullet points that show the benefits of retro running to those *so lame* "backward" forward runners

But retro runners also do it for the glory, as showcased in races held on six continents.

Though people have been "backing that thing up" for thousands of years, the sport gained some popularity in the United States in the early twentieth century and some extra notoriety in the 1980s after Robert K. Stevenson published *Backwards Running*. In 2008, Italy hosted the first official backward marathon, along with the second world championships.

It's not as if runners invented the idea of going backward. Women in ballroom dancing have performed nearly the same steps as their partners, but backward, *and in high heels*—and they never brag about bonus cardiovascular points. The same is true for rowers, backstrokers, scullers—and even some pole vaulters, high jumpers, divers, parachutists, flipping boarders, Michael Jackson–moonwalking imitators. . . . So, retro running amounts to a *new* civilization?

> "Maybe, if there were more mixed sports—for example: figure skating, acrobatic rock and roll, sports dance, mixed gymnastics, mixed synchronized swimming, or alternative mixed running—there would be more communication and unity between men and women and by extension, more friendship, more love and more harmony in couples on the earth. The alternative mixed running is the next step of athletics for the next millennium."

—Christian Grollé, retro running promoter

If alternative mixed running—a forward-running man and a retro running woman, then with reversed roles—doesn't solve relationship issues, it's worth giving counseling or sex another shot; quoting less from *Backwards Running* in the bedroom might also help.

## Getting Back to the Starting Line

Here's a look backward at the advances retro runners have achieved in the past several decades.

**2007:** Roland Wegner of Germany sets the record in the backward 100-meter dash with a time of 13.6 seconds.

**2004:** Thomas Dold of Germany runs the backward mile in a time of 5:47 minutes. (Just to compare, the "forward" mile world record is 3:43.13 minutes, currently held by Hicham El Guerrouj of Morroco.)

**1990:** Yves Pol of France travels 99.4 miles in twenty-four hours, establishing the record for the farthest distance traveled backward in a single day. Talk about going nowhere fast.

**1984:** Arvind Pandya of India completes a 107-day backward run across the United States, racing 3,169 miles from Los Angeles to New York City.

**April 15, 1931–October 24, 1932:** Over eighteen months, Plennie
   L. Wingo of the United States takes an 8,000-mile backward walk,
   a record distance.

For more on how retro running is moving backward into the future, see
www.backward-running-backward.com.

## Retro Cycling Records

While this may seem to be about the satanic messages supposedly
embedded in "Stairway to Heaven" and other rock bands' records—messages that could be revealed by spinning the vinyl in reverse—it's not.
That's back*masking*, and this is backward *cycling*, which, by the way, is
an effective treatment in reha-
bilitating athletes with serious
knee injuries.

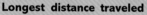

   These athletes must possess knee joints with the
stamina of a jackhammer. And
remember, all these feats are
performed facing backward
on a cycle zooming forward.

**Longest distance traveled
   in one hour:** Markus Riese (Germany, 2003): 18.1 miles
**Fastest 50 kilometers** (just over 31 miles): Markus Riese (Germany,
   2003): 1:46:59 hours
**Fastest 100 kilometers** (62.1 miles): Alan Pierce (Australia, 1985):
   4:05:01 hours
**Longest distance traveled on a *motorcycle*:** Hou Xiaobin (China,
   2006): 93.21 miles

# Retro Cycling

Unlike retro running, no one claims backwards cycling "will provoke a fundamental questioning of our commonest attitudes" or "bring about the social change that the urgency and gravity of the problems of our day require." It may, however, give you handlebar marks on your butt.

Yes, riders sit on the handlebars, rather than the seat, and pedal backwards. In order to tell where he or she is going, some backwards cyclists swap out the seat for a mirror, while others use forward-riding friends, acquaintances, or even perfect strangers, to direct them—or misdirect them, in order to put goofy pictures on their online gallery.

Scotsman Sebastian Tombs did have friends—lots of them, in fact—assisting the 58-year-old to navigate a 60-mile canal in Edinburgh backwards for AIDS research in 2008. The United Kingdom's University of Derby also holds an annual 45-mile backwards ride between the university's Buxton and Derby campuses; in 2008, there were 70 entrants, including a reverend and a university administrator on a tandem.

But few can rival violinist Christian Adam's world record: In 2007, he rode backwards for nearly 38 miles, while wearing a tuxedo and playing Bach on his violin. And few would want to.

> **"It was quite tricky, I remember, and did result in a lot of injuries."**
>
> —Backward cyclist Sebastian Tombs

# "If hell has a suburb, it looks like this."

*—Wall Street Journal*

What good is a lawn mower if it's buried behind the tangle of garden tools, the dog's outgrown crate, the Exercycle with the missing seat, and all the other accumulations that the seasons change from storage to wreckage, from thriftiness to plain mess?

But if *that* mower seems useless, what if, like fanatics from England, Australia, and forty-five U.S. states, you remove the grass-cutting blades so you can race your machine, thereby turning "a weekend chore into a competitive sport"? To paraphrase a few of the racers' spouses: "Only a man could come up with something like this."

An English rally-car racer, frustrated by the rising costs of his sport, debuted the event in 1973: Lawn-mower racing offers an inexpensive, accessible event with no lingering misgivings about whether to bag your clippings. Today, the British Lawn Mower Racing Association hosts several events, including the British Championship, World Championship, and 12-Hour Endurance Race—that's enough time to mow something like 36 acres!—without clipping a single blade of grass.

The U.S. Lawn Mower Racing Association, started in 1992, hosts between ten and fifteen races each year, including the STA-BIL Keeps Gas Fresh Finals and Challenge of Champions in Delaware, Ohio, and a season-long points race, in which mowers with painfully punning names such as Ace of Blades and the Bat Mowbile "get the mow on the road."

From stock classes to highly modified classes, some mowers chug along at 6 to 8 miles per hour (even after a few brewskies, most any Sunday-afternoon mower could race one of these), others lean into turns at 35 to 40 miles per hour, and still others reach speeds of up to 85 miles per hour. Talk about getting your mow-jo on.

Think you can outrun (or outpun) these bladeless runners? Mow for it at www.letsmow.com or www.blmra.co.uk.

**Other Names of Actual Lawn Mower Racers**

Mr. Mow Jangles, Geronimow, Mowron, Sodzilla, Turfinator, Prograsstinator, Hedge Hog, Weedy Gonzales, Mr. Mow It All, Mowdacious, Yankee Clipper, Mowertician, Precious Mowments, Lawnsome Dove, Mowna Lisa.

# "Tiller pilots . . . must wear shoes."

—World Championship Rotary
Tiller Race rule book

According to the Pur-
pleHull Pea Festival in
Emerson, Arkansas (pop-
ulation 359), the Wey-
erhaeuser 200 World
Championship Rotary Til-
ler Race is the "highlight of the tiller-racing season." Considering it's the only
tiller race around, the "Tiller Thriller" is indeed a highlight. And if you're looking
for peas—purple-hulled peas, in particular—you've come to the city that "pays
homage to this wonderful tasty legume with its itinerant and historic past."

The event is not named for the number of laps, but for the length of the
track: It's all of 200 feet. Since 1990, competitors have plowed into races of
two sorts: **stock,** where the tillers are driven just as they come from the factory,
and **modified,** where racers can "run what you dare." There are eight divisions, none of which manage to churn the ground into a humus-rich crumble
for successful planting:

**overall stock:** Any racer, age five to fifty-five, can compete with an unmodified
tiller of at least 3 horsepower.

**youth stock young men:** The stock rules apply here, but the competitors are
all boys seventeen and under. Despite their prowess with a tiller, none has
yet to cultivate growth on their own chests.

**youth stock powder puff:** Another stock division, but for girls seventeen and
under, none of whom would trade a mirror and blush for the natural glow
that a nice dusty run across a field brings.

**super-duper dirt slangers:** Competitors are eighteen and up, and they race modified tillers of at least 100 horsepower, equipped with a "kill switch" that connects the ignition of the engine to the rider's wrist. Each machine's steel tines must show "some resemblance of digging or slinging dirt." The world record in this 200-feet race: "Wild Thang" Wayne Waller, with a time of 6.12 seconds.

**rip-roaring tillers of the '90s:** In this "true" tiller modified class, machines run through a tiller gearbox (transmission) and can reach speeds over 20 miles per hour. The world record here: Shane Waller flew across the 200 feet in 5.72 seconds, averaging 24 miles per hour.

**ladies' modified:** Women may run a "dirt slanger" or "rip-roaring" tiller, providing they have "proof of a recent mental examination."

**flower-bed tillers (little men):** These are stock races using 2-horsepower tillers for boys ten and under. All boys must have successfully demonstrated that they can take care of their radish-sprout-in-a-paper-cup school project in order to enter the competition.

**flower-bed tillers (little ladies):** Same thing, but for girls who are willing to race without putting streamers on the tiller's handlebars or a basket in front so their favorite stuffed animal can race, too.

Ready to dig in? Visit www.purplehull.com/TillerRace.htm.

**"Equal parts
snow, speed
and courage ...
sprinkle in
a little insanity,
stir well with
a shovel."**

—John Strader, www.shovelrace.com

As the saying goes, when the snow comes down, you have two choices: Shovel or make snow angels. It's probably clear why ski-lift operators and trail-maintenance workers came up with a third

alternative, and it wasn't making a tape loop of Irving Berlin's "White Christmas" to broadcast across the slopes. Instead, they decided to ride their shovels down the mountains when they got off work and created a new sport. Their first champion-ships were held in the

1970s in Angel Fire, New Mexico, further inspiring precocious children to leave their sidewalks half-cleared and ride their little scoops down the driveway into the street.

The winter Olympic sports are "elitist," says veteran shovel racer John Strader: "We're a working man's sport. Every truck driver in America has a shovel in the back of the truck. . . . We're the poor man's luge."

Control is the biggest issue in **traditional shovel racing,** which is performed on a standard-grain scoop shovel, with the pilot sitting in the bucket, the handle extending forward like a tiller. But the handle, precariously positioned between the legs and in a straight line with the face, isn't used for steering: Riders drag their hands to keep their shovels on a true course.

One other factor is crucial for successful shovel racing: waxing the shovel, which, depending on the rider, might mean actual wax (ski or car), Teflon, or lunchmeat—ham is the most popular.

Racers can also compete in two other classes, with **light-modified** or **super-modified snow shovels.** These "vehicles" use nitrogen-filled pneumatic braking systems, along with independent hand and/or foot brakes, yet no one has actually figured out an effective way to stop someone going 72 miles per hour on a shovel. Riders can risk pulling up on the shovel handle while using their feet to stop; "go corpse" (lie flat to decrease speed); or, as any self-respecting athlete would choose, crash.

The light-modified shovel resembles a street luge, weighs under 100 pounds, and does not require a roll cage or harness (super-modified does). Recklessly reaching top speeds of 74 miles per hour, this modified shovel is completely impractical for digging a rider out from an unplanned burial in snow.

Known to insiders as a "cross between a soapbox derby and a bobsled," super-modified racers are shovels that weigh between 100 and 500 pounds and can blast down slopes at 79 miles per hour. This souped-up class also requires that the shovel touch the snow within 12 inches of the rider's butt, and that said rider must have at least two people present to vouch for his sanity before and after the race.

Strader's super-modified snow shovel resembled a torpedo with a windshield on the outside and a NASCAR cockpit on the inside. It was equipped with a protective roll cage and five-point harness safety belt. Creating the biggest spill on a hill since Jack and Jill's legendary fall, Strader's shovel tumbled out of control at over 70 miles per hour, twisting and flipping like an Olympic gymnast; it left him with a broken back, broken leg, and internal bleeding. But it was the sport itself that took the biggest hit; the modified shovel races were canceled from competition after Strader's spill at the sport's X Games debut in 1997, forcing the X Games to choose sports that gave competitors a reasonable chance of walking away without—well, without an inability to walk. Never to be seen on ESPN again, the sport continued to hold its world championships until they, too, were nixed in 2005, forcing shovel racers to return their "vehicles" to their previous use, when late-for-work spouses called from their cars, "Can I get a hand here? I'm stuck in the driveway."

Looking for the inside scoop? Check out www.shovelrace.com.

# "Never squeeze your cups."

—Advice from World Sport Stacking Association

"Will you just do the dishes already?" Steve Purugganan's mother must request impatiently, as her son rapidly constructs pyramids with the dinner glasses instead of scrubbing them with the soapy sponge. The ten-year-old World Sport Stacking Association Champion then probably leaves the kitchen to watch reruns of himself on ESPN2.

Dominated by a recent graduate of the sippy cup, sport stacking (formerly known as cup stacking) was invented at the Southern California Boys and Girls Club in the 1980s before receiving national attention on *The Tonight Show Starring Johnny Carson* in 1990.

Stackers begin with 9 or 12 inverted cups, "up stack" them into pyramids, and then "down stack" them into the original stacks, maintaining the original sequence. The basic 9-cup formation,

called "the 3-3-3 stack," involves assembling and disassembling three 3-cup pyramids. Mr. Purugganan can do this in 1.86 seconds; that's about the time it takes the rest of us to just grab one paper cup from the dispenser beside the water cooler. In the basic 12-cup stack, called "the 3-6-3 stack," the task is to build up and break down one 3-cup, one 6-cup, and another 3-cup pyramid. There's also 12-cup cycle stacking, plainly enough called "the cycle stack," that goes: one 3-6-3 stack, one 6-6 stack, one 1-10-1 stack, and then a final down-stacked 3-6-3 formation. Purugganan holds the overall world records for these events as well, with times of 2.34 seconds and 6.21 seconds, respectively. (Right about now, you should be wondering about the countless ways in which you wasted your youth. . . .)

Stackers compete in individual events, relays, and even doubles events in which teammates stack simultaneously, one using the right hand, the other using the left. WSSA-sanctioned competitions exclusively use plastic Speed Stacks® cups, which contain three holes "to allow air to escape quickly while down stacking" to increase speed. They also have a textured exterior "for a terrific feel and grip"—something the rest of us look for in a baseball glove or a chef's knife.

To avoid "tippers," "sliders," "topplers," or "slanters"—ways in which a cup can fall, according to the vast lexicon of stacking terminology—

the WSSA suggests never passing a cup from one hand to the other and "allowing gravity to do the work on your down stacking." Plus, intentional distraction or interfering with an opponent's cups results in a forfeit, so moms have to leave their bullhorns and sore feelings of unattained personal athletic stardom in the minivan.

Though there *are* adult divisions, including collegiate (ages nineteen to twenty-four), masters (twenty-five to thirty-four, thirty-five to forty-four, forty-five to fifty nine), and seniors (sixty-plus), the sport is geared toward children (age divisions by year for twelve and under), so the "stacked" jokes are clearly off-limits. Plus, the four and under competitors are arguably the cutest things ever, having only recently let go of Mom's bra cups.

Half empty? Half full? Who cares at www. worldsportstackingassociation.org, where the rule book begins, "We only build positive pyramids!"

**"Puzzles may be made smoother internally by sanding or using any lubricant."**

—World Cube Association regulations

Erno Rubik, Hungarian inventor, sculptor, architecture professor, and inventor of the Rubik's Cube, once said:

> Space always intrigued me, with its incredibly rich possibilities, space alteration by (architectural) objects, objects' transformation in space (sculpture, design), movement in space and in time, their correlation, their repercussion on mankind, the relation between man and space, the object and time. I think the CUBE arose from this interest, from this search for expression and for this always more increased acuteness of these thoughts.

To which everyone within earshot responded, "Yeah . . . for *you,* maybe."

Fortunately for the 263 competitors representing thirty-three countries at the twenty-fifth Rubik's World Speed Cubing Championship in Budapest, learning to pronounce *növelt élesség* (Hungarian for "increased acuteness") was not a prerequisite.

There was, however, **blind cubing,** in which blindfolded, fourteen-year-old Hungarian Matyas Kuti solved eighteen successive cubes in just over forty-six minutes, disproving the age-old adage "Keep your eyes on the cube."

There was the **foot-solving event,** in which another old adage "You know what they say about big feet . . . " failed to help competitors in the least.

And then there was the **classic 3x3-cube event:** The overall winner, sixteen-year-old Yu Nakajima, solved five consecutive cubes in an average of 12.46 seconds.

What separates champion cubers from those of us who thought the cube, along with slap bracelets and women's shoulder pads, disappeared in the '80s, is not just knowledge, but practice. For example, Andrew Kang, who once solved 3,800 cubes in a day, became the U.S. Rubik's Cube champion while still in high school. He typically practiced cubing three to six hours per day, which still left him plenty of time to solve life's other puzzles, such as finding a college with a Rubik's Cube major.

Kang also recommends:
- Lubricate your cube.
- Examine the cube ahead of time, and try to discern patterns in the puzzle.
- Solve the puzzle layer by layer (think: three-layer cake) rather than side by side (don't think: dozens of cupcakes).
- Remember that edges remain edges, corners remain corners, and center squares maintain their relationship to one another.

"A lot of people think it's a gift that some people can learn things faster than others," Kang says, "but it's just a matter of how much effort you put in." Skipping two meals a day to practice should suffice.

---

### Speed-Cubing Simulation

Cubers work with tremendous velocity *and* precision, because they're penalized if any layer of a solved puzzle is even slightly misaligned. To get a better idea of this speed and dexterity—such as solving the classic cube in a world-record time of 7.08 seconds, like Erik Akkersdijk of the Netherlands )—try this simple test.

1. Make sure you are alone.
2. Now, hold your hands out in front of you as if you're holding a Rubik's Cube.
3. Twiddle your fingers as fast as you can, occasionally flicking your wrists as if you were turning the cube.
4. Once you've finished solving your imaginary puzzle—perfectly aligning the colors on each face—place it on the table, stand up, look around to make sure you're still alone, throw your hands triumphantly into the air, and congratulate yourself.

While this test may give you some sense of the dexterous speed with which cubers actually work, you're now about as qualified to compete in one of the hundred World Cube Association annual events as your air-guitar sessions are to earn you a chance to sit in with Metallica.

---

To solve a Rubik's Cube, you merely need to find the one correct configuration out of a total of 43,252,003,274,489,856,000 possibilities. Need more advice?
See www.worldcubeassociation.org.

# three

## Recess Gone Wild

Most of the time, those brief breaks on the playground didn't even involve sports: You were either rubbing the mulch out of your eye, sitting beside the teacher on duty for shooting juice-box straws at lunch, or building a Death Star out of Legos for the fourth rainy day of "indoor recess!"

And when you *were* playing those games designated for that twenty-minute period of postlunch euphoria, did you ever picture a game of rock, paper, scissors worth $10,000, or a 25-foot-tall swing set? Did you ever propose finger-wrestling your friends, Bavarian-style? (Probably not, since the only European nations you could name were probably Greenland and Hawaii.)

While some of the sports in this chapter do honor their ties to the playground—as far as we can tell, tunnel tag and Red Rover are still confined to those twelve and under—others have jumped the school-yard fence and, with one untied shoe, run willy-nilly halfway across the sporting world.

Take, for example, nol-ttwigi, a Korean variation of seesaw: Instead of sitting on opposite ends of the board, two girls stand, bounce each other many feet into the air, and perform acrobatic flips and twists before landing to return the favor. In Malaysian gasing, both children and adults spin tops weighing 11 pounds, either trying to knock over their opponent's tops or to keep their own spinning for as long as possible; the record spin is over two hours.

Oh, to be a kid—or to merely act like one: Time just seems to fly!

## "High to the clouds without drugs."

—Motto of the Estonian Kiiking Union

At your neighborhood park, you might expect to find redheaded twins playing "chicken" on the monkey bars, a frustrated nine-year-old inching down the way-too-sticky slide, or a pair of lovebirds arguing over who gets to hand the jump rope back to the lady from Parks & Rec. What you might not expect is a European man on the swing set who can wheel riders who are standing on the "seats" over 25 feet high in a complete 360-degree circle over the spindle. The sport of kiiking, Estonian for "swinging," is hardly child's play.

Each swing is made of telescopic carbon steel and has arms that can be lengthened from

3 to 8 meters (about 10 feet to over 26 feet). Since 1999, the Estonian Kiiking Union has sanctioned competitions where participants defy
gravity and their loved ones' wishes by using their weight, a pumping-
squatting motion, and the *oomph* of momentum to swing until they can
make a single rotation over the crossbar. In competition, the height of
the swing's arms is lengthened little by little; the winner is the one who
makes it over the bar with the longest swing arms.

Kiiking as a recreational activity dates back to the nineteenth century when partygoers in Estonian villages would ride four- to ten-person timber swings, some of which are still in use today. Unlike the kiikers on today's metal swings, earlier swingers were not harnessed in (hands and feet bound to the poles and platform, respectively). What's Estonian for "Look, Ma, no brains"?

**In competitions, each athlete has a maximum of five minutes to propel the swing over the bar, yet few competitors can manage longer than three minutes. The leg muscles are quickly exhausted with that forceful deep-knee bending, squatting, thrusting, pumping motion.**

If we're talking semantics, it's worth mentioning that while *kiik* is "swing," many aficionados of the sport say you're not really kiiking until, while swinging, your legs are reaching higher than your head. If we're talking statistics, then you'd need to know that Andrus Aasamäe holds the kiiking world record with a 7.02-meter swing (over 22 feet). The American record—5.31 meters—is just short of the women's world record of 5.86 meters. First it was baseball, then basketball, and now kiiking: What's happening to America's athletic dominance?

Speed and height make kiiking an adrenaline-pumping sport. According to www.kiiking.ee, "woman in a skirt on the swing" makes it a spectator one.

## "Right hand, left hand, two hands forehand, and two hands backhand . . . for one minute each . . ."

—What each player must hit in a team rally speedball competition

Speedball, if nothing else, holds the honor of possessing the sporting world's most generic name. It does beat alternatives such as "ball-on-string hitting game" or "spherical object of high velocity." And "racquetball" was already taken. So in 1961, tennis coach Dr. Mohamed Lofty of Egypt invented speedball, a game where one or more players use a small plastic racquet (just larger than a table tennis paddle) to whack a ball tethered to a rope around a pole. It's tetherball for the really, really coordinated. It's what lifeguards do as they spin their lanyard around a finger, back and forth for forty-five minutes until rest period, but with a ball instead of a whistle.

Also popular in the United States, Europe, and Japan, the sport is governed by the International Speedball Federation. Apparently not a fan of irony, Lofty's apple-size latex ball often travels upward of 120 miles per hour, ensuring that the game does indeed involve not only a ball but also speed.

Speedball is played in one of four actual games, although many players of other racquet games use speedball as a way to practice hundreds of swings without having to chase after hundreds of balls.

## Supersolo (one player)

- Played on a 4x4-meter court. It's an athletic sort of solitaire.
- Players (that would be you) go for as many hits as possible in four one-minute intervals, with a break between each.
- Players must hit four kinds of shots: right, left, two-handed fore-hand, and two-handed backhand.
- Egyptian Nabil Imam holds the world record of 575 hits in four minutes. That's an average of 2.4 whacks of the racquet every single *second*.

## Singles (two players)

- Played one-on-one on a 6x4-meter court.
- Players (that would be you and a date) alternate serves as well as forehand and backhand serves.

- A player scores a point if the ball turns twice around the pole before his opponent hits it.
- The game is played to 10 points; a match is best of three games; and a date is something other than swatting a ball around a pole.

## Which Speedball?

It's key to know your audience when speaking of speedball. The name is shared by any number of other sporting and nonsporting things:

    an injection of cocaine and heroin
    a road rally
    a nonspiking volleyball game favored in India
    coffee with added espresso
    a combination handball/soccer game
    a small punching ball used in boxing
    a videogame
    a comic book character with the powers of kinetic energy
    a brand of ink and pens with interchangeable nibs
    a rock band
    a paint-ball game with bunkers

## Doubles (four players)

- Played on an 8x6-meter court.
- Think maypole dance, but without the pretty streamers or the dance.
- Players must alternate serves and hits during a point.
- Additionally, players try not to hit one another in the face.

## Team Relay (four players)

- Here there are four players per team, who play one at a time.
- Each player hits for thirty seconds, then another comes in immediately.
- Teams go for as many total hits as possible.
- The ball continues to whirl around the pole—think revolving door, spinning very fast—as each player dives into play.

At www.worldspeedball.org, you've got the world—and a 120 mile-per-hour ball—on a string.

# "The world record holder first competed to win a box of fudge."

—www.prostoneskipping.com

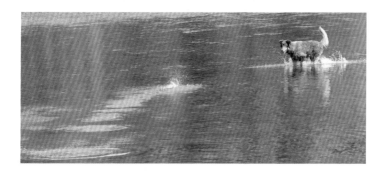

Pennsylvanian Russ "Rock Bottom" Byars skipped a stone an incredible fifty-one times. It traveled approximately 250 feet and sank right into the *2007 Guinness Book of World Records*.

Stone skipping (called "ricochet" in France, "stone skiffing" in Ireland, "smutting" in Denmark, or "ducks and drakes" in England) has been around since the advent of water and stones. (In point of fact, some accounts suggest that Moses skipped the broken tablets across the water after he came back from Mt. Sinai and saw the heathens.) Still, it took until 1989 for the North American Stone Skipping Association to establish its bylaws. Today's largest competition is the World Stone Skimming Championship in Easdale Island, Argyll, Scotland, which attracted over 220 competitors from eleven countries in 2007. Though American events, such

as the Mackinac Island National Tournament, record the number of skips, skippers at the championships in Scotland compete for distance; the record—65 meters (about 213 feet)—was set by Australian Iain MacGregor in 2001.

While there is no perfect size or shape of stone, Byars recommends his "submarine" technique: He throws side-arm, uses his index finger to increase spin, and attempts to hit the water at a 20-degree angle, proving once again that it's not the size of the stone, it's how you use it. That, and, according to Rock Bottom, "stretching with a golf club, drinking coffee, and prayer."

Ready to "rock" on the water? Skip over to www.prostoneskipping.com.

**"All you need is an arm and a wrist and fingers. It is best to wear loose fitting clothes ... Pregame stretching and manicures are strongly encouraged."**

—World RPS Player's Responsibility Code

According to a new documentary on competitive Rock, Paper, Scissors, the sport is "a combination of Halloween, Mardi Gras—really, a *Star Trek* convention with binge drinking and much better-looking women." The World RPS Society also offers another description: "The Wimbledon of lazy, drunk decision-making. Imagine Agassi if he loses, goes to the bar, gets shit-faced, and then comes back and heckles the guy who beat him."

Despite such self-deprecation, less-than-sober hilarity, and bountiful unsportsmanlike conduct, the society has established its very own Responsibility Code; among other things, it advises competitors to "establish what is to be decided or whether the match is to be played for honor."

They've also created a new lexicon (see chart on page 68)

WORLD ROCK PAPER SCISSORS SOCIETY
Above All
Nothing beats Rock!

out of the twenty-seven possible "gambits," or three-move sequences
in the game that has been "serving the needs of decision makers since
1918." Despite your neighborhood's own version, to win a competition RPS tournament, the best two of three throws wins a set, and the
best two of three sets clinches the victory. And while they may govern
what appears to be the dimmest negotiating tool this side of One
Potato, Two Potato, both USARPS and the World RPS Society have also
devised strict rules, with penalties given for invented throws such as
the chimerical "live long and prosper," the devilish "Texas longhorn,"
and the ineffective but potentially offensive "I've got your nose."

RPS tournaments are held internationally, including the USARPS
Championships, sponsored by Anheuser-Busch, which features tournaments in bars nationwide that produce regional winners, who eventually
compete in Las Vegas for a $50,000 prize. The world championships,
where the winner pursues a share of the measly $13,000 purse, are held
in Toronto and attract able-fingered competitors from countries as distant
as Norway, Australia, and Singapore, all of whom consider themselves

THE CHOICE IS YOURS

World RPS Society

PAPER

"ambassadors of the World RPS Society." (All that international détente for naught!) But no matter how high the stakes, the society advises players to "think twice before using RPS for life-threatening decisions."

Visit www.worldrps.com or www.usarps.com, where they remind us all that "recycled paper still beats rock."

## The Gamut of Gambits

RPS, when used to decide who gets to ride shotgun or who has to make the naked lap around the parking lot, provides more than a few opportunities for humor. So do Graham Walker and his colleagues at World RPS, who defined these gambits and concluded they were "the most historically significant and widely employed" of the twenty-seven possible three-play combinations. For instance, The Denouement—rock, scissors, paper—"relies on a cooling-down approach to gently destroy your opponent." Or The Bureaucrat—paper, paper, paper—whose "dead-pan delivery . . . is the ultimate in passive-aggressive play." Here are a few others to consider for your next meet.

| | | |
|---:|:---:|:---|
| rock, rock, rock | = | **The Avalanche** |
| paper, scissors, rock | = | **The Crescendo** |
| rock, paper, paper | = | **Fistful o' Dollars** |
| paper, scissors, scissors | = | **Paper Dolls** |
| scissors, scissors, scissors | = | **The Toolbox** |

**"To the beginner the choices are few, to the expert the choices are many."**

—Wojek Smallsoa, *The Trio of Hands,* 1962

**So, who gives a spit?**

Some things you can't wait to get out of your mouth: baby teeth, orthodontia, a jumbo shrimp gone over to the dark side of ammonia. But there's an entirely different category of oral expulsion: the world's assemblage of salivary-greased, lung-powered, expectorated tidbit competitions. You know . . . spitting.

So why would you want to participate in such sports, when there are so many other more noble contests?

Maybe it's because you shouldn't have put whatever it is in your mouth to begin with: Unlike much of the population, contestants at the Prune Pit Spitting Festival in Sainte Livrade sur Lot, France, actually enjoy the shriveled fruit.

Maybe it's because your uncle *wasn't* lying about a swallowed seed growing an entire plant in your stomach: Corn-kernel-spitting contests are held at town festivals around much of the United States.

Maybe it's for health reasons: A contestant at the National Tobacco Spitting Contest once explained, "Get your juice right. It can't be too thick or too thin. You've got to just chew for about an hour and not drink or eat anything and get your mouth adjusted to it. Then it's slick and smooth and just comes out easy." This was before such competitions ended in the 1970s.

Or maybe it's the competitive spirit itself, with the accompanying purse: Winners of the Watermelon Seed Spitting Contest in Luling, Texas, receive $1,000, the largest prize for any palatal performance.

For whatever reason, spitting contests continue to gain popularity. Here are a few favorite feats of spittoonery.

## Crickets

**"Cricket must remain intact, and an official must check the spat cricket for six legs, four wings, and two antennae before the spit can be counted."**
—Rules of the Purdue University Bug Bowl

Big 10 schools are known for their sports: Ohio State Buckeye Archie Griffin won back-to-back Heisman Trophies. Tom Izzo led Michigan State to three consecutive Final Fours. Dan Capps, competing at Purdue, spat a dead cricket more than 32 feet.

At fifty-one, Capps was hardly a frat boy when he established his record. Nonetheless, the Wisconsin native traveled to the land of the Boilermakers to compete in the cricket-spitting contest at Purdue's Bug Bowl, an annual entomological extravaganza established in 1996.

Brown house crickets are the preferred projectile. Each weighs between 45 and 55 milligrams—about the weight of a quarter-carat diamond but not nearly as sought after on engagement rings.

The crickets are frozen and then thawed just prior to the competition. Although a contestant must spit within twenty seconds of placing the cricket in his or her mouth, many employ the Capps Technique, emulating "the way his tongue curls pinkly, and folds wetly around the cricket, coating it with saliva before each spit."

Fellow Big 10 school Penn State also holds an annual spit-off. Slowly but surely, cricket spitting may work its way up the conference ladder, one day filling all 107,782 seats at the university's Beaver Stadium, the largest in the nation.

## Cherry Pit

**"Hopefully, you get a nice round one."**

—Brian "Young Gun" Krause

Father-son time traditionally involves heading off to a baseball game, spending a day at a pay pond, or sitting at the kitchen table trying to figure out why sonny-boy keeps bouncing checks when his checkbook shows— well, that it hasn't been balanced since leaving for college.

But for Rick "Pellet Gun" Krause and his son "Young Gun," known as Brian at the top of his checks, winning the International Cherry Pit Spitting Championship is real bonding time.

Held since 1974 at the Tree-Mendus Fruit Farm in Eau Claire, Michigan, the championship has belonged to Pellet Gun ten times, along with the world record flight of 72 feet 7 inches. The spitting image of his father, Young Gun has now claimed the title seven times since 1993, and spat a cherry pit 93 feet 6½ inches, making his father's previous record look as ignorable as a maraschino cherry on a cocktail garnish.

As champion, Young Gun received an apple tree that was dedicated in his honor and planted in the orchard, a free hotel stay at the following year's competition, and some "remember-when-I-used-to-let-you-win" joking from dear old Dad on the ride home.

## Kudu Dung

**"There are many ways to spit the pellet, although all of them, of course, involve putting a piece of dung in your mouth."**
—Project Galactic Guide

"Dung" is something of a euphemism for the absolute last thing a person would ever consider popping into his or her mouth. Perhaps the word lowers the threshold of revulsion. Perhaps it lowers inhibition. Perhaps it doesn't.

Nonetheless, at the World Kudu Dung Spitting Championships, competitors fearlessly spit kudu feces. ("Feces" is a slightly less euphemistic euphemism, while "kudu" is a euphonious name for a type of African antelope.)

Still, according to one blogger with firsthand experience, "even the most die-hard of competitors is unwilling to put a fresh pellet in his mouth, as this is just plain disgusting." Rather, he says, the dung "must be firm, not crumbly, otherwise the pellet could break up in the mouth, resulting in a bad aftertaste, and the ridicule of the other competitors."

The origins of kudu dung spitting, also known as *Bokdrol Spoeg*, are humiliating to humans on many levels. The kudu, a notoriously difficult animal to hunt, was infamous for leaving a trail of its dung pellets while managing to elude hunters. In response, hunters began using the pellets in spitting competitions to "retaliate" at their prey. (Readers: If you *are* interested in gaining revenge on someone, please note that putting his or her shit—euphemism deliberately withheld—in your mouth and spitting it out is entirely ineffective.)

So if polite words don't get you participating, and if vengeance isn't motivating, you'll want to try what the competitors use: Mampoer, good ol' South African moonshine.

| Spitting Distance | | |
|---|---|---|
| **Who?** | **Spit what?** | **How far?** |
| Brian "Young Gun" Krause | cherry pit | 93 feet 6½ inches |
| Lee Wheells | watermelon seed | 68 feet 9⅛ inches |
| Shaun van Rensburg | kudu dung | 51 feet ⅗ inch |
| Serge Fougère | prune pit | 43 feet 2 inches |
| Dan Capps | brown cricket | 32 feet ½ inch |
| George Craft | tobacco juice | 24 feet 10½ inches |

Croquet rhymes with "play," as in, "Care to play croquet? The lawn has been freshly mown and my whites, nicely pressed!" It does not rhyme with "sweat," as in, "Croquet, like golf, is designed for those who shun the very idea of breaking into a sweat." (*Croquette*, that little crunchy fried morsel, does rhyme with "sweat," and so ends today's French lesson.) The epitome of backyard recreation, the sport gained popularity in England in the mid-nineteenth century and arrived in America once there was cargo room on the ships for discretionary items such as brightly colored wooden balls.

In the basic game, players alternate shots, using a wooden mallet to hit the ball through a course of wickets arranged on a closely cropped, weed-free lawn. Once a ball is shot through all the wickets, it must strike a final stake before completing the course in reverse. Points and extra shots are awarded for scoring wickets, finishing in the least number of shots, and roqueting—that is, knocking away other players' balls with a satisfying, "I am *owning* this game!" After the game, some players have tea and crumpets, use the word "jolly," and continue to perpetuate what Americans consider British stereotypes.

Ah, but once things leave merry old England, they rapidly gain street cred: Take, for example, Thomas Paine, David Beckham, The Beatles, and such croquet corruptions as:

**Toequet,** in which players kick a soccer ball through enlarged wickets

**Golf Croquet,** ideally played on a "green," where points are awarded only by scoring an individual wicket before your opponent

**Bicycle Croquet,** a cycling version of the game where players swing their mallets while riding

Sure, these, along with the other croquet variations below, may have evolved from a British import, but they're a helluva lot more respectable than quoits or skittles.

## Extreme Croquet

**"Roqueting Another Player's Beer or Respective Drink Results in Two Extra Turns. Nothing Is Obtained for Hitting Your own Drink—Other Than a Berating From the Other Players for Wasting Precious Resources."**
—from the San Francisco Extreme Croquet guidelines

Extreme-, eXtreme-, or simply Cross-Country Croquet had its beginnings in the 1920s, when a Long Island man constructed a croquet course that included sand traps, bunkers, and "rough." Long Island being one of the least eXtreme places on Earth (have you ever seen it spelled lOng Island?), a name wasn't given to the sport until a Swedish club commandeered the game in 1975. But it took the founding of the Connecticut eXtreme Croquet Society in 1984 to rally American attention to the game, which it describes as "an intensely aggressive game, where the phrase 'safe shot' has no meaning."

Noted for outlandish rules and even more outlandish playing fields, extreme croquet is typically held in one or more of three favorite venues:

**woodland areas:** See this section's title for an apt description.

**stream beds:** What sport *can't* be improved with splashing, decaying leaves, and the chance to find crawdads?

**railroad tracks:** This is only slightly less safe than just setting up the wickets on the Autobahn.

The CECS ensures that all playing fields are oddly shaped with irregularly spaced wickets. Their courses span between 50 and 80

yards, depending on the season, although some courses have ranged over 125 yards with wickets placed where "if you overshoot the shot by 3 feet, you drop off a ledge. . . ."

In San Francisco, the resident club hosts annual tournaments with competitors nicknamed Captain Kangaroo, Dr. Punish, and Steak Boy. They have especially strict rules regarding, for instance, a sudden outburst of song during play: "There shall be no singing of—or in the style of—show tunes on the course. Offending players will be verbally berated and threatened with physical violence." Should you take a shot out of turn, there are repercussions: You must move your ball back to its previous position, "wait in shame for your turn," and bring cold refreshments and apologies to "all the players whose balls you stroked out of turn."

Watching these extreme malletheads, you might start wondering whether they're playing crack croquet.

For East Coast players, check out www.extremecroquet.org. West Coasters, see www.extremecroquet.com.

## Mondo Croquet

### "If your ball splits into multiple pieces . . . finish the game with the largest piece."
—Mondo Croquet organizer's manual

In the history of sports, time seems to enlarge things: numbers of participating teams, salaries, opportunities to shill stuff. Is it any surprise that the Oregon city that advises itself to "Keep Portland weird!" would upgrade to Mondo Croquet, which uses 16-pound sledgehammers and bowling balls for their games? "Leave mallets and wood to the marimba!" they say. (Wait—no, that's what we say.)

Each year at the Mondo Croquet World Championships, players use bent steel rebar as wickets and Portland's annual Mad Hatter Picnic as an excuse to dress like elves, princesses, and the top hatter himself.

The stake at the far end of the course is topped with a stuffed animal, and the starting and ending stake is topped with a skull or skeleton. (Why, you ask? Once a player completes the course and hits the start/end stake, his ball becomes a "zombie" and can eliminate other balls by striking them.) If the game were to gain popularity in

---

### Hot Shots

At Seattle's Lakewood Croquet Club, the motto is "Mallets plus morons equals mayhem." (Remember that one for the next time you're hunting for a needlepoint pillow design or a temporary-tattoo idea.) Not only does the club possess an affinity for alliteration, but members also condone cheating; they train their dogs and children to move the balls to the owner/parent's advantage. And they speak in "grating approximations of British accents" during play, using a lexicon all their own for innovative shots that include:

**The Shuffleboard Shot:** Probably the most widely used move, it's a variation of a shuffleboard shove. The player sets up low to the ground, often on his or her knees, and slides the mallet along the ground, striking the ball with the flat top of the mallet (rather than either of the two striking surfaces). This shot "butts" the ball, to create an accurate hit across a short distance.

**The Pool Shot:** Yep, this one is carried out like a billiards shot. The ball is struck by the handle-end of the mallet. The shot is ideal for when a player wants to "jump" his ball over an opponent's ball.

**The Corkscrew of Death:** A shuffleboard shot with flair. The player first holds up the mallet, spins it quickly in his or her hands, and yells out, "All must fear the Corkscrew of Death!" in his or her best British accent.

Hollywood, we'd be seeing trailers for the next blockbuster, *Zombies with Sledgehammers*.

While Mondo Croquet players do exhibit genuine fortitude by wearing Raggedy Ann–striped stockings in public, they do not possess balls of steel: If a player cracks his ball, he must finish the game with the largest piece. Unless, of course, he buys beers for the entire crowd.

Feel like a "big shot" already? All the weird you need is at www.mondocroquet.com.

"**Splashdiving is . . .
a community
for girls, boys,
and especially
freaks.**"

—www.splashdiving.com

We've all seen a sixteen-year-
old, 4-foot-11-inch, 85-pound
Olympic diver execute
a flawless 2½
somersaulting
dive with 1½
twists (degree
of difficulty 3.4, for
those who are counting),
falling from 10 meters (about 33 feet) and traveling
over 25 miles per hour, only to enter the water like a raindrop—
a prepubescent Chinese raindrop, the sort you hear plink-plinking
on your acupuncturist's sound track.

If the Summer Olympic Games ever decided to hold an Opposite Day, German splashdiving (or *Arschbombe,* which translates—not even loosely—as "ass bomb") would be a featured event. Not only are competitors rewarded for the size and volume of their intentionally explosive splashes, but the creators of the official championships have even concocted genuine nomenclature for those lackadaisical terms such as "can opener," "pancake," and "cannonball" twelve-year-olds use to try to grab the attention of the foxy high-school lifeguard by soaking her up in the chair. (Actually, "cannonball" did join their new global lexicon, as you can see in the chart.)

With cosponsors such as Fanta, Nestlé, Mitsubishi, Speedo, and Mentos (which has even given its name to the Mentos Fresh on Tour competitions), the sport now attracts divers from several European countries, Australia, and the Philippines—the smack of cold water against bare flesh must be a kind of Esperanto.

Platform splashdivers execute stylistic and complicated midair somersaults and twists, but with off-balance, skewed, and torqued techniques. Basically, the more you veer from Olympian grace and alignment, the more your onlooking family cringes, the crowd roars, the points escalate, and your bellysmacked flesh reddens.

As divers get better and better (what sensitive-to-pain observers call "worse and worse"), they move up the Bombing Bounce, a ranking system with levels that include hopper, jumper, diver, master, champion, and baron. (Ah, just like the learn-to-swim levels . . . pollywog, turtle, minnow, porpoise, and, finally, whale. So why isn't "whale" the pinnacle of splashdiving talent as well?)

Many baron splashdivers also perform **exhibition dives.** Three-time world champion Christian "Elvis" Guth once jumped 25 meters (about 82 feet) from a crane. For true bash brothers, there is also the **synchro competition,** along with junior events for boys overly eager to say they're "master barons" in polite company. To train, most athletes begin by splashdiving from the pool edge of a splashdiving-friendly neighborhood *Schwimmbad.* According to the official splashdiving Web site, "a public pool suitable for Splashdiving must meet the following criteria: Diving platform; allow Splashdiving."

Although the rules for practicing aren't stringent, according to Australian splash-diver Joey Zuber, in order to be a champion, one must possess "the pain tolerance of the Germans. . . . They don't feel anything in their arses!"

Looking to sew a new patch on your swimsuit? Join the bombing bouncers at www.splashdiving.com.

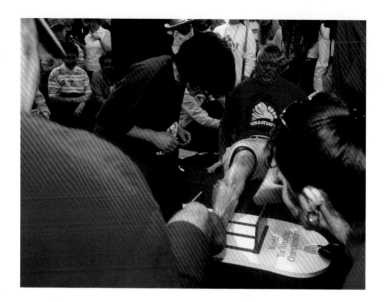

Real wrestling often involves cauliflower ears, skinned knees, floor burns, bloody lips, sprains, pains, strains, dislocated joints, and embarrassingly attentive parents with camcorders in the front row of the bleachers.

Fake wrestling often involves something like blood, smoke machines, daily manscaping, folding chairs, sequins, shouting matches, choking noises, stomping, slapping, slamming, and high pay-per-view prices.

Praise be to the gods and goddesses of grappling, nobody *really* loses in toe wrestling (there's zero chance of being body slammed from the top turnbuckle) or in finger wrestling, where there's free beer!

## Toe Wrestling

**"There's no 'arm' in toe wrestling."**
—The sport's official motto

Every year, competitors from as far away as the United States, Canada, Australia, and Germany travel to the Bentley Brook Inn in Ashbourne, Derbyshire, England, for the world's least furtive and most aggressive game of footsie: the World Toe Wrestling Championship.

While the day begins with a comprehensive toe and foot inspection of all competitors, the same cannot be said for the puns. According to George Burgess, who resurrected the sport in 1990 (it disappeared in 1977), toe wrestling comes down to "perseverance, ankle strength, and having a 'toe-riffic' sense of humor."

Competitors sit on a "toedium," place their feet on a wooden frame called the "toesrack," interlock the big toes of both feet, and face off in a best-of-three "toe-down," trying to push their opponent's feet off the frame. If a wrestler is in too much pain, he or she may forfeit by calling, "It's toe much!" adding insult to injury.

In 2005, Paul "The Toeminator" Beech and his wife, Heather "Mrs. Toeminator" Beech, took the men's and women's titles, respectively. Paul defeated Alan "Nasty" Nash, who had won five consecutive years, including 2000, when he had an "undisclosed broken foot." Meanwhile, Heather went toe-to-toe with her sister and defeated her in the women's final. When it comes to toe wrestling, apparently many things are "relative," including a sense of humor and toe size: Bigger ones are more winning.

# Bavarian Finger Wrestling

## "You have to have a fat finger, so that the strap has a good hold."

—Veteran finger wrestler Anton Utzschneider

Finger wrestling, or *Fingerhakeln,* is said to have settled disputes in the Alps as early as the seventeenth century. Why not actual wrestling, you ask? Was it that no one wanted to soil their lederhosen (those Oktoberfest leather shorts, suspenders, and knee socks)? Was it because their Tyrolean hats (think: Peter Pan) are easily flattened?

Instead, at the Bavarian Finger Wrestling Championships in Germany and at Austria's Alpine Championships, the sport's only injuries include some skinned fingers or the occasional dislocation. Sitting on opposite ends of a table, competitors chalk up, hook middle fingers in

Outside of Bavaria, wrestlers share in the difficulty of finding worthy opponents.

a tough leather strap, and attempt to pull their opponent out of his seat and onto or over the table.

Some wrestlers train by doing pull-ups with only their middle fingers. Some use only their digits to lift over 100 pounds. Others merely enjoy rounds of *Weizenbock* (7 percent to 10 percent alcohol content), and consequently make good use of the "catchers," who protect competitors should one be pulled hard enough to fly completely over the table.

### Ready to Rumble? You'll Need:

1 leather strap just under 4 inches long and just over ¼ inch wide
1 table that's about 31 inches high x 29 inches wide x 43 inches long
2 stools that are 15¾ inches tall
2 competitors ready to give each other the finger

# four

## Mix-and-Match Sports

Combining sports generally yields disaster. Mix up two physical sports, such as judo and soccer, and what do you get: kickball? Pair two more rudimentary sports—a little backyard catch and a no-blinking contest: You've got little more excitement than someone with a bloody nose. Even twining two of our greatest national pastimes is risky: Ever see the 1998 box-office flop *Baseketball,* the cult movie with the curious distinction of featuring the first sport to "promote poor sportsmanship"?

And what could possess a community, a few retired coaches, or college kids on winter break to braid elements of three, or even four, sports into one "hairy buffalo" of potent athleticism?

And yet, in some instances, the whole of *some* sports can be greater than their totally random, inane, nonsporting, or even unsportsmanlike parts. In this chapter, we take a look at sports that have seized— or is the expression "laid siege to"?—some of your favorite games, least favorite games, or activities such as yogic breathing or household chores, which never in their wildest fantasies dreamed of being a game. Then we throw them all in a blender, add some blood, sweat, tears, ice, and alcohol (optional), and serve up some truly mixed-up mishmash 'n' mayhem.

## "The equivalent of beer-league wiffleball in the ice-bound sports world."

—The credo of The Flock, a team in the Evanston Broomball League

Tired of lacing up your skates, but love the idea of ice? Broomball's for you, the sport that's always trying to distance itself from the "I'm with stupid ➜ " T-shirt worn by its cousin, curling, where athletes push granite rocks shuffleboard style across the ice, while two guys with brooms sweep the surface in front of the ball to direct its path onto a bull's-eye.

In the early 1900s, before *Fantasia* revealed that all brooms are possessed, streetcar workers in Canada used their brooms to hit a small soccer ball to pass the time when winter winds must have discouraged passengers from climbing aboard an open trolley car. Over the years, broomball has come to resemble ice hockey, played on a rink with six members (five plus a goalie) on each team.

Contrary to curling tradition, and despite what its name might lead you to believe, broomball doesn't involve brooms. Sure, back in the day, a broom's bristles were frozen, dipped in rubber, and wrapped in tape, but today, players are much happier wielding a wooden or aluminum shaft with a triangular rubber head. (If only the rest of us could be made happy so readily.)

Broomball's creators must have concurred that pucks are too hard and that skates only remind players why they're so bad at hockey, so broomball players use an orange rubber ball about the size and color of an inside-out cantaloupe, and get to wear a pair of waterproof sneakers, specially designed for ankle support and traction.

Since the 1960s, organized leagues have "swept" across Australia, Japan, Italy, Germany, Switzerland, and twenty-six cities in the United States. The International Federation of Broomball Association hosts the biennial World Broomball Championships, leaving curling out in the cold . . . with all those chilly folks who let the trolley cars pass them by.

Ready to come out of the broom closet? Visit www.usabroomball.com.

In tenth-century Iceland, a sport similar to broomball known as knattleikr pitted one village against another in games that lasted up to two weeks. Waged almost like a war, the competition frequently resulted in casualties. Considering such high entertainment value, many are still surprised, eleven centuries later, that Iceland's top attraction is whale watching.

> **"Referees
> have a whistle,
> microphone,
> various percussion
> instruments, and
> a DJ set."**
>
> —From www.bossaball.com

American beach games include flicking your beer's lime wedge between the goal posts of your two feet at the end of your deck chair, or "first-one-to-crispy" tanning races. Some beachgoers venture to the sand volleyball net before taking a nap at the first sign that "glow" is turning to perspiration.

But in South America and Europe, beach athletes grab that volleyball for a sport that's equal parts "soccer, gymnastics, and *capoeira* (an acrobatic Brazilian martial arts form)," mixed up on a court of trampolines and inflatables, and served with a cranked-up bossa nova soundtrack (fruit garnish, optional). Yes, bossaball pretty much kicks sand in the face of beach paddleball.

Created in the early 2000s by Filip Eyckmans, a Belgian living in Spain, bossaball matches two teams of three, four, or five players on an inflatable volleyball-sized court, with a built-in trampoline near the net on each side. (Once again, we ask: What sport *wouldn't* be improved with the addition of a few trampolines?) Players serve with either hands or feet, and teams may hit the ball up to eight times per side. Each player can hit the ball consecutively twice with his feet or head, but only once with his hands.

Teams generally use all eight touches per side to allow the attacker, the team member on the trampoline, to bounce to maximum height (up to 12 feet), before setting him up for a spike. One point is scored if the ball hits the ground on the opponent's side; three, if it lands on the trampoline. If a player digs the ball before it touches the ground, or if the ball hits the bossawall—the inflatable barrier surrounding the court—the point continues.

With its disco-fever personality and definite portability (the entire court sets up in forty-five minutes), bossaball is getting crowds "bouncing" at music festivals, dance clubs, and beach parties in numerous countries throughout South America, Europe, and Asia.

Meanwhile, here at home, Americans ride mechanical bulls, take mosh-pit elbows to the chest, and continue to perfect field goals with lime wedges.

Want to be the boss o' the ball? Bounce over to www.bossaball.com/english.html.

# "The thinking man's contact sport."

—Motto of the World Chess Boxing Organization

Did you ever imagine that a comic book could inspire an international sport? (Don't pretend that you never read comic books and can't answer the question.) Dutch artist Lepe Rubingh brought to flesh and blood a game featured in a 1992 French graphic novel, and held the first Chess Boxing match in 2003, helping to legitimize the new sport, as well as his own reputation, by fighting under the nickname "The Joker." *WHAM! KAPOW! Checkmate!*

What's *not* exactly comical is falling victim to a knockout or, just as potent, the loss of your king in the sport where, according to the World Chess Boxing Organization, "fighting is done in the ring, and wars are waged on the board."

Chess boxing matches begin with a four-minute round of what's known as "speed chess": Each competitor is allotted twelve total minutes in the match to move his pieces. After the chess come three minutes of boxing, after which there is a one-minute break for athletes to trade gloves and mouthpiece for a towel and headphones, which block out crowd noise and the arena's PA system, where a commentator is explaining to the crowd that "the little horsy piece" is actually called a knight. Then, trying to avoid mistakes caused by pumping

---

### Do-It-Yourself Mind 'n' Body–Sport Generator

Here, for readers ready to think outside the batter's box, is a chance to imagine the next new sport. Choose any item from the first column, add any item from the second column, and then suggest a new name for your competition. We've supplied a few to get you started.

| Thinking Man's Sport + | Contact Sport = | Your New Sport |
| --- | --- | --- |
| Hangman | chicken fighting | Kung Kapow Chicken |
| mixology | mixed martial arts | Mixed Mini-Mart |
| New York Times Sunday crossword puzzle | sumo wrestling | Weight, Weight, Don't Tell Me |
| Chinese Checkers | hide and seek | Losing your Marbles |
| spelling bee | spelunking | Spell 'n' Spill |
| Lego construction | pogo-stick jumping | Going to a Go-Go |
| Scrabble, tic tac toe, Old Maid, Chutes and Ladders, debate, checkbook balancing, memorizing decimals of pi, Go Fish, mah-jongg, Texas Hold 'Em, Wheel of Fortune, instant poetry, Pictionary, reciting the Gettysburg Address, fortune-telling, naming all the state capitals | racquetball, pole-vaulting, hammer throw, whitewater rafting, bobsledding, balance beam, archery, ostrich racing, snowboarding, pommel horse, discus, figure skating, tower diving, karate, quiots, steeplechase, t'ai chi, power lifting | [this space for your sport names or for doodling] |

adrenaline or a hook to the jaw, it's back to the board. The match can take up to eleven rounds (six of chess; five of boxing) to decide a winner, either by knockout, points, checkmate, or disqualification for exceeding the twelve-minute chess time limit.

The official WCBO rules also stipulate that "If a game of chess ends in a tie, it is settled with the points earned in a boxing round. If the boxing fight ends in a tie, the player who had black on the chessboard wins."

While the WCBO recommends contenders be proficient in both disciplines, they also suggest a training regimen that includes Chess Boxing sparring; 400-meter chess (eleven rounds of a lap around a track alternating with three-minute "blitz" chess matches); and gong chess (punching the sandbag for three minutes; hitting the chess board for four).

Think these guys can't be serious? Not just any "Joker" can step into the ring. To qualify as a chess boxing fighter, a competitor must have a minimum of twenty boxing matches under his belt, plus an ELO (the international boxing rating system, named after its creator, Arpad Elo) of at least 1800, which places a chess player in Class A, one level beneath expert status. Speaking of classes, some German elementary schools are even teaching the sport these days. No joke.

Want to become a right-roundhousing, bishop-blitzing champion? Utilize both brains and brawn at www.wcbo.org.

"A bicycle kick in soccer . . . [is] a really rare occasion . . . but in sepak takraw, you see it almost every volley."

—Daniel Angerhausen, secretary-general of Germany's sepak takraw association

"Volleysoccernastic footbag" has a certain ring to it, but it didn't win out as the final name of this sport. "Sepak takraw" did; *sepak* is Malaysian for "kick," and *takraw* is Thai for "woven ball."

Originally played as a cooperative circle game similar to hacky sack, the sport dates back to the 1400s, although it wasn't until 1965, at a debate at the Southeast Asian Peninsula Games, that "sepak takraw" emerged as the sport's accepted name. Prior to that, it was called "takraw" in Thailand; "sipa" in the Philippines; "ching loong" in Myanmar; "rago" in Indonesia; "kator" in Laos; and in still other places, "foot volleyball." Today the game is simply "takraw" in the USA, which is shorter than volleysoccernastic footbag but not a whole lot more pleasant rolling off the tongue.

Wildly popular in Southeast Asia, the game combines key elements of three games: volleyball's goal of landing a ball over a net onto the opponent's side, soccer's no-hands policy, and gymnastics' somersaulting and acrobatics. Some say that martial arts would be the game's fourth element. Net footbag *could* be considered the sport's fifth element, but then it would sound like that Bruce Willis movie.

In a takraw game, two three-person teams, or *regu*, face off kicking, heading, and kneeing a hollow, woven, synthetic-fiber ball that's slightly larger but just lighter (and definitely softer) than a softball, over a 5-foot-high net. Teams try to get the ball to land on the ground of the opponent's side and to prevent it from hitting the ground on their own side, but each team may touch the ball only three times before putting it over the net. While it *is* legal for one player to take all three

touches, just as one may hog all the meatballs on the family-style platter of spaghetti, it's not the best policy, as all the best takraw players understand (although they make the analogy using a platter of *gai pad khing*, Thai ginger chicken).

To begin a point, one player tosses the ball in the air to the *tekong*, or server, who kicks it to the other side. The *tekong* stays in back, while the two others work the frontcourt: One is the "passer," who sets up the "killer" for an acrobatic mid-backflip or a mid-somersault spike that sends the ball traveling up to 80 miles per hour—or, if you're Thai superstar Suebsak Phunsueb, nearly 100 miles per hour. The game's "telegenic oomph," as *Time* puts it, comes from the long rallies, athletic spikes, and dramatic in-flight showdowns as a spiker and defender soar above the net to challenge each other on almost every play.

Despite Phunsueb's skill and celebrity, Thailand's world dominance is always challenged by Malaysia, which makes for epic matchups at the Asian Games and King's Cup World Championships. Along with nearly every Southeast and East Asian nation interested in besting "Thai" in the world rankings, serious competition has been building in several European countries, Brazil, Iran, Canada, and the United States, which hosts its annual U.S. Open in Minnesota. Can you even get *gai pad khing* in St. Paul?

Looking for a sport where you can still be a real player? Join Takraw USA's "15 to 20 members who are serious and dedicated" to the sport at www.takrawusa.com.

**"They picture you running the course with red hair, floppy shoes, and a red nose. But you have to cross the finish line with a ball in the air."**

—Joggler Albert Lucas

Jogging does not require great skill: You just try to run *not* fast.

Juggling, on the other hand, does require both considerable skill and the lack of whatever gene it is that makes most folks blush with embarrassment when even *thinking* of making a spectacle of ourselves in the name of family entertainment.

Despite the two sports' apparent disparity in skill level and entertainment value (unless the jogger is aflame, a celebrity, or, the *real* star, a flaming celebrity!), devoted enthusiasts have combined the two and christened it with a portmanteau of its very own: joggling.

Now quit your scoffing: Joggling was an actual Olympic sport until 1932. (Quit scoffing, really! The Games at one time also included tug-of-war and live pigeon shooting.) And today, joggling has understandably seized the attention of Americans who are juggling work, freelance jobs, their kids' lacrosse and ballet practices, their spouse's habitual lateness, and finishing their book club's novel while switching channels among Sunday play-off games.

Jogglers, who generally use three or five balls and occasionally pins, must maintain a consistent juggling pattern while running. If a joggler drops a ball, he must return to where it fell and get the balls back in the air before continuing. (Reader: If you still find sophomoric ball-dropping jokes amusing, here is a perfect place to add your own.)

The International Juggling Association Festival Championships hold a variety of joggling competitions, including **sprints, hurdles, distance,** and **relays.** While many competitors actually complain of their hands going numb, juggling doesn't seem to slow them down as much as you might expect. The joggling record for a mile—4 minutes 42

seconds—would have broken the regular mile world record . . . um, for *women* . . . women in *the 1960s* who could run incredibly fast.

The joggling **marathon** record of 2 hours 50 minutes 9 seconds qualifies for the Boston Marathon, with almost 20 minutes extra to poke around Quincy Market, chase dropped balls, or think of more ball-dropping jokes. Joggler Perry Romanowski endured a 50-mile **ultra marathon** in 8 hours 23 minutes 52 seconds. We have to believe that for some time afterward, Romanowski refused to be on his feet while holding anything heavier than a 250-count bottle of Aleve. But the man proclaimed "Greatest All-Around Juggler in the Twentieth Century" by most everyone, including the *Guinness Book of World Records*, is Albert Lucas. Juggling since the age of three (teething rings, Cheerios, sporks), at ten, Albert was the youngest performer on *The Ed Sullivan Show*. (Talk about prodigies: Mozart never even made it onto TV, let alone *Ed Sullivan*!) Currently, Lucas possesses over thirty joggling gold medals (he quit counting long ago), holds the world record for number of objects juggled at once (thirteen rings), and continues an amazing streak: He's never dropped a ball in a single race.

Still scoffing? Well, go on then, invent your own portmanteau of a sport! Become the first to try . . . scroggling or joffing or jaggling.

Feel like jogging your brain with more joggling blogging? Check out Perry Romanowski's "Just Your Average Joggler": www.justyouraveragejoggler.com.

> **"A player shall not attempt to stifle a raider's cant\* by shutting his mouth or throttling."**
>
> —International Kabaddi Federation

Curiously, some of childhood's greatest games revolve around the potential of having a collapsed lung: Taking a clothesline to the sternum from a pair of prematurely pubescent fifth-grade titans during a game of Red Rover; doubling over, completely winded, as you officially prove yourself the slowest kid at tag; or succumbing to your big sister's challenge of "bet I can hold my breath longer than you" before discovering that her puffed cheeks were only distracting you from the fact that she was breathing through her nostrils. Kabaddi combines the joys of all three bronchiole-busting competitions!

---

\* A cant, which according to some experts is a corruption of the English word "chant," is the continuous repeating of the word "kabaddi" in one exhalation. Kabaddi raiders develop greater lung capacity through this form of *pranayama*, or breath control.

Hindi for "holding of breath," kabaddi is a combative seven-versus-seven competition. Teams score by having a single player from one team "raid" the anti-raiders (simply called "antis") of the defending team, who form a chain by holding hands. (Picture a vise grip, not a walking-in-the-rain-with-someone-you-love grip.) The raider's goal is to tag as many opposing players as possible without getting caught—all in the span of one breath, one slowly exhaled breath that chants the game's name, "kabaddi."

If a raider tags an anti, the team of antis attempts to tackle or block the raider so he'll take a breath and lose his cant. Tagged antis, along with raiders who lose their cant, are eliminated from the game, awarding a point to the opposition. When one team eliminates every opposing player, all players on both teams return to the game. After forty minutes, the team with the most points is declared the winner and breathes a deep, deep, not-particularly-yogic sigh of relief; the losing team attempts to hold its collective temper.

Played on an area similar in size to that of half-court basketball, kabaddi is not a frenetic game. Rather, cat-and-mouse-like strategies dominate as raiders slowly line up an attack while chains of antis circle. The action is quick and decisive: A raider quickly accelerates. He thrusts

a hand to an opponent's chest. He kicks at an anti's legs. Anti chains immediately surround the raider. There's a point! There's another! Raiders are even talking of *extra* points for defeating a group of Nazi antis en route to the lost ark!

The national sport of Bangladesh, this South Asian game is said to have been played by Siddhārtha Gautama, the founder of Buddhism, as early as sixth century B.C. and apparently sprung from a method of warding off group attacks.

In the modern era, the 1936 Berlin Olympics presented a demonstration of the game. Although Hitler's opinion of kabaddi was not recorded, we can almost guarantee that it was more favorable than his legendary snubbing of Jesse Owens. The Amateur Kabaddi Federation of India was founded in 1972 and the sport debuted at the 1990 Asian Games. Today, the Kabaddi World Cup features teams from India, Pakistan, England, Canada, and the United States. Ironically, the round-bellied Buddha himself would now be disqualified: Players must weigh less than 80 kilograms (176 pounds).

Haven't felt like holding your breath until you turn blue since you were six? Vanquish your inner tantrum at www.kabaddiikf.com.

"**Any garment is suitable, but it must be at least the size of a tea towel. It's hardly impressive to iron a handkerchief.**"

—Extreme Ironing

After a long workday at an English knitwear factory, Phil Shaw didn't feel like ironing his clothes, but he did manage to muster the energy to go rock climbing that evening *and* iron his clothes at the same time. (It's that clean-your-plate-and-*then*-you-can-have-dessert motivation that we try to teach our kids.) Thus, in 1997, the birth of extreme ironing, "the latest danger sport that combines the thrills of an extreme outdoor activity with the satisfaction of a well-pressed shirt."

Since then, extreme ironists have taken their wrinkled garments both high (Mount Everest) and low (the Blue Hole off the Egyptian coast), both north (the North Pole) and south (Antarctica)—and most everywhere in between (for instance, across a gorge at the Wolfberg Cracks in South Africa). There's hardly a global

## Build Your Own Extreme Ironing Event

Customize your own steaming adventure by choosing one element from each of the three columns —they're all taken from EI's archives of documented feats.

| Basic Action | Outfit or Gear | Location |
| --- | --- | --- |
| climb in a go-kart | wearing a tuxedo | into an ice cave in Mich. |
| set off in a whitewater raft | sealed inside a full SCUBA suit | down to the Blue Hole off the coast of Egypt |
| slide down a zip line | crowned by a birthday hat | atop Mount Everest |
| roll on your skateboard | covered by a Speedo | across Trafalgar Square |
| ride a tandem bike | playing a guitar | at a castle in Wales |
| pulled by water skis | wrapped in a diaper | to soak in a hot tub |
| race downhill on a snowboard | outfitted in a wedding dress | at the North Pole |
| hang glide | camouflaged in military fatigues | in the Sahara Desert |
| stand atop a moving Jeep | breathing by snorkel | inside the Eiffel Tower |
| leap into the aisle just as the pilot turns off the "fasten seat belt" sign | sporting a Jesus-style, hair-beard combo | at London's Streatham Speedway |
| set your ironing board ablaze | bundled in a fur-lined anorak and mukluks | on the continent of Antarctica |
| spring into a handstand | outfitted in vintage bellbottoms | amid a Welsh bog |
| straddle an illuminated gas-station sign | tattooed from head to foot | out in Death Valley |
| hop on the bike rack of a moving taxi | wearing nothing but your birthday suit | above the presidents on Mount Rushmore |

destination that hasn't been subjected to their not entirely un-ironic pressing.

Shaw, or "Steam," as he's been nicknamed, created the Extreme Ironing Bureau in 1999, which validates record-breaking attempts and sanctions EI events, such as the Rowenta Tour, during which the world's best practitioners embark upon an extreme ironing crusade across a country or continent.

According to the official rules, to break a record, one must photograph or record themselves at an outdoor landmark, with a 1-meter long, 30 centimeter-wide ironing board with legs, along with a "real" (non-plastic) iron. Plugs, or even extension cords, are hardly necessary; these athletes are more involved in pressing their luck.

The bureau has sections in New Zealand, South Africa, and the United States, with an estimated thousand people participating in extreme ironing worldwide. The German Extreme Ironing Section hosted the world championships in Munich in 2002, an event at which eighty participants competed.

Sure, ironing while BASE jumping or paragliding, or during a 30-foot dive off the coast of Melbourne in a seventy-two-person team (a Guinness World Record–breaking feat in 2008) might get you mentioned in sports blogs or printed on a poster, but it probably won't help you make a nice straight crease in your shirt's pleats. Not to worry, says the EIB: "There are occasions where the danger and the thrill of extreme ironing are more exciting than the actual ironing."

Feeling a little hot under the starched collar? Get out there and iron! See www.extremeironing.com.

# "Mud. Bikes. Tears. Pain. Cyclocross: an hour in hell."

—Anonymous cyclocross competitor

Remember that first time you got up on your two-wheeler, your new red three-speed bike, when Dad, scooting along to help you gain momentum, finally thrust you forward, letting you ride with your own balance, wind rushing past your face, butterflies fluttering in your belly . . . ?

And remember how quickly you lost control, swerving into the neighbor's stupid bed of petunias and marigolds with that big fancy rock in the center that's still streaked red where your fender grazed it as your tire popped? Remember how the neighbor shouted from the front door that she had already phoned the police as you walked your bike back to Dad crying, "Why did you shove me so hard?"

Remember?

As if riding through a suburban obstacle course weren't tough enough, one sport takes bikes to terrains so treacherous that sometimes competitors can't even navigate the course while riding. Cyclocross, invented in the early 1900s when European road racers took off-road shortcuts through farmers' fields or over fences getting to the next town, is an "off-track" bike race, where riders try to maintain some kind of speed across pavement, wooded trails, sandpits, plank barriers, and other obstacles. When the cycling's impossible, or when running with a bike slung over your shoulder would be faster, cyclists quickly dismount and become runners for up to 10 percent of the course, which is normally between 1½ and 2½ miles.

This is a sport with international appeal: France held its first Cyclocross National Championship in 1902; seventy-three years later, so did the United States. The world championship, held since 1950, brought fifty thousand competitors to Treviso, Italy, for the 2008 Union

Cycliste International Cyclo-Cross Championship. Due to the hazardous conditions, expert riders compete with modified bikes, a pit crew with extra equipment, and a spare bike—an understudy bike, as it were, that sits in the wings waiting for its big break. With all that grassy terrain, graveled stretches, and steep hills, it's tough to figure why competitors don't consider bringing a backup Jeep.

Love running? Love biking? (Not so crazy about swimming?) See if cyclocross is your kind of triathlon at www.cxtreviso2008.com.

---

### **What the Riders Have to Say**

"'Cross is like the antithesis of road riding."

"Every lap, there are a hundred things to get right, a hundred things to get wrong."

"It's everything your mother said you couldn't do as a kid."

"It's like a steeplechase with bikes."

"It makes a bike race as stupid as possible."

# five

## Now, Tell Me You're Not Actually Going to . . .

Oddly, idiocy seems to have a permanent position in sports. How many times have you heard commentators berate a player (out of the athlete's earshot, of course, and insulated by the fact that the player is *playing* and not listening to the broadcast) about "a stupid foul," "a bonehead play," or "a fall must have rattled his brain" moment? Now imagine entire games based on little more than gut feelings and unruly rules.

These sports, which range from the belligerent (say, shin kicking, where even realizing you won't be able to walk the next day isn't enough to kill your buzz), to the dangerous (in winter-swimming contests, the one shared prize is instant hypothermia), to the borderline illegal (at *El Salto del Colacho,* Spaniards leave their babies on mattresses in a street for costumed men to leap over).

Yes, these are the sports that have EMTs on standby, mothers on pins and needles, and clergy encouraging spectators to pray for the participants' dear demented souls. (Sounds like preaching to the choir to us.)

But for these athletes, such events are nothing shy of heaven on Earth.

"Swimming across the pool and pushing 'icebergs' out of my way, it was time to get out."

—Extreme cold-water swimmer
Paul Hopfensperger

### Hot or Not?

When it comes to sports, extreme heat encourages competitors to remove clothing: fewer layers, lighter fabrics, skimpier uniforms, more skin exposed, greater interest from cameramen. Surprisingly enough, so does extreme cold.

It's true: Some do like it hot. The rest, on the other hand, drink Brass Monkeys, Blue Tits, and Chilly Willy (the three specialty beers served at the Winter Swimming Championships). The 850 swimmers there compete in:

- a **cold-water race:** That's your basic 25-meter (82 feet) sprint in your basic ice bath.
- an **endurance event:** That's 450 meters (1,476 feet) of shivering and mind-over-what's-the-matter concentration.

- **artistic competitions:** Teams with three to twenty swimmers offer two- to five-minute performances, "preferably humorous," that may include costumes, music, and storylines while in water that hovers just above 32°F.

If you're the sort who prefers to just plunge in and get it over with as quickly as possible, you're out of luck: Diving is prohibited; there's a high likelihood of experiencing cold shock, which is a world of pain worse than sticker shock. In fact, putting one's head underwater is illegal; only the "head-up breaststroke" is permitted at the championships, and all swimmers must wear a hat or cap to hold in body heat, a great deal of which escapes through the scalp.

After each race, swimmers immediately retrieve their clothes, take warm showers, and attempt to revive their own blue tits and brass monkeys. Despite the temporarily detrimental physical effects of cold-water swimming, many regular competitors claim improved circulation, stronger immune systems, and, in fact, an increased desire to warm up their own chilly willies.

Feeling frigid? Want to increase your libido? Check out www.slsc.org.uk.

> "When you first jump in, your skin is absolutely burning. You also experience massive hyper-ventilation, so coordinating the breathing with the swimming stroke is really difficult. Because I swim the crawl, I often gasp in a little bit of water. After five or ten minutes you start losing the feeling in your fingers and toes, and as it slowly moves up your legs, you notice how inefficient your stroke is becoming. Then you have this feeling of miserable, aching cold, deep inside you. That's probably a good time to get out."

—LGP

# Profile in Cool:
# Lewis Gordon Pugh

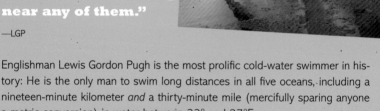

> "I have encountered crocodiles, hippopotami, sharks, polar bears, leopard seals, and jellyfish. I don't enjoy swimming near any of them."

—LGP

Englishman Lewis Gordon Pugh is the most prolific cold-water swimmer in history: He is the only man to swim long distances in all five oceans, including a nineteen-minute kilometer *and* a thirty-minute mile (mercifully sparing anyone a metric conversion) in water between 32° and 37°F.

Pugh is also a solid candidate for a future *X-Men* movie—no special effects are even necessary: He's the only person ever recorded with the mutant power of anticipatory thermogenesis! While not as sexy, perhaps, as telekinesis or metamorphosing into various beasts, he has a conditional response that allows him to elevate his body temperature simply by standing at the edge of cold water. (Mere humans merely shake, dip a toe into the water, and wonder why they chose the Maine shore over Miami Beach.) This means that Pugh—who routinely gains between thirty and forty pounds before undertaking a swim—begins the day at 98.6°F and dives into subzero water with a 101.2°F fever.

When he's not busy pounding down the calories for a frigid-swim weight gain, Pugh serves as a maritime lawyer and leading global environmentalist. Evildoers—Magneto, toxic waste-dumpers, polluters—watch out.

Thinking of going for a dip, just Pugh and you? Take the plunge at www.lewispugh.com.

## "This is how hell must feel."

—Sauna Heinola, the organizing body of the World Sauna Championships

The best competitions make leisure into sport, like turning an afternoon of watching flicks into a movie marathon. In Finland, where there are 1.5 million saunas (there's one for every 3.33 Finns), the organization of World Sauna Championships did just that with the first competition in 1999. Annually, over 160 competitors from nearly twenty-five countries travel to Heinola to see who can endure the longest, hottest sauna.

Competitors enter the sauna in small groups, and every entrant must assume the same position: seated erect, buttocks and thighs on the bench, forearms on the knees, and arms upright; hands may touch no other part of the body. Turns out, a 230°F wooden box that grows hotter every thirty seconds as water is poured onto the sauna's stove can make a person look as if "a waffle iron had been repeatedly pressed" against the skin, as one competitor described it. As heat and steam increase, there's less and less oxygen to breathe: Indeed, it's *not* the heat, but the humidity that drives competitors from the sauna.

One other competition bylaw: "Disturbing the other competitors in any way is strictly forbidden," although it's tough to imagine anyone making jokes about "not knowing your heinie from Heinola" after 18 minutes 15 seconds—Finn Bjarne Hermansson's winning time in the 2008 competition.

Think this competition sounds like no sweat? Think again at www.saunaheinola.com.

# *Actually,* It's Not the Heat, It's the Stupidity

This customized thermometer, in degrees Fahrenheit, should help you appreciate the chilling nature of these temperature-taunting athletes.

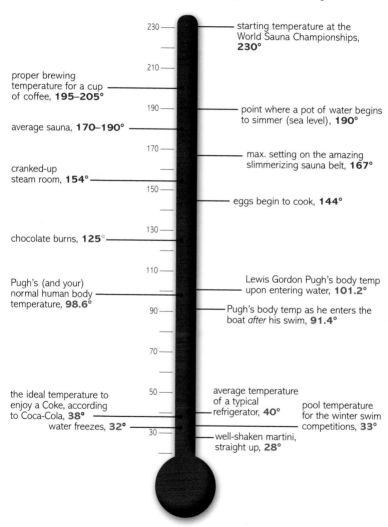

starting temperature at the World Sauna Championships, **230°**

proper brewing temperature for a cup of coffee, **195–205°**

point where a pot of water begins to simmer (sea level), **190°**

average sauna, **170–190°**

max. setting on the amazing slimmerizing sauna belt, **167°**

cranked-up steam room, **154°**

eggs begin to cook, **144°**

chocolate burns, **125°**

Pugh's (and your) normal human body temperature, **98.6°**

Lewis Gordon Pugh's body temp upon entering water, **101.2°**

Pugh's body temp as he enters the boat *after* his swim, **91.4°**

the ideal temperature to enjoy a Coke, according to Coca-Cola, **38°**

average temperature of a typical refrigerator, **40°**

pool temperature for the winter swim competitions, **33°**

water freezes, **32°**

well-shaken martini, straight up, **28°**

> **"[There's] zero visibility . . . rather like swimming in bug-infested soup."**
>
> —Bog Snorkeling official Web site

At the annual World Bog Snorkeling Championships, a charity event held since 1985, almost 170 competitors test the waters of the Waen Rhydd Bog in the small Welsh town of Llanwrtyd Wells. True, "Waen," "Rhydd," and "Llanwrtyd" do sound like words bubbling out of a snorkel—but that's understandable, considering swimmers aren't allowed to have their heads above water for anything more than a moment of orienteering as they race to complete two lengths of a 60-yard peat bog channel. Those with self-respect (and a more than passing interest in winning) generally wear a wetsuit, along with the required snorkel and flippers. Other competitors don inflatable sumo suits, military camouflage, tea dresses, or even a nun's habit. So how hard could the championships be?

"A lot harder than I expected," one curvaceous man in a flouncy skirt admitted, "especially carrying a handbag."

Purse or no purse, competitors inevitably look ridiculous while dog-paddling (conventional swim strokes are illegal) through the bog's thick slime and muck, complete with the occasional newt.

Of the worldwide entrants who arrive for the Wales's Bank Holiday event, most are avid swimmers or play underwater hockey (page xxx). Some are just kids (the minimum age is fourteen). Others are just kidding (one snorkeler made the grungy plunge in his footie pajamas). Some are far from kids (one woman competed in celebration of her seventieth birthday). Still others are all about winning.

"I have got to be good at something," said Iain Hawkes, who didn't graduate from the U.K.'s equivalent of high school or college. "But I *am* the champion of bog snorkeling," the 2008 winner proclaimed. Sure, Hawkes took the 2008 title, but his effort wasn't enough to toss Joanne Pitchfork's world record time of 1:35.18 minutes from its algae-strewn, moss-covered throne.

Can't imagine getting bogged down in Wales? What about in Northern Ireland or Australia, where they also host championships? For more, visit www.green-events.co.uk or www. bogsnorkelling.com.

Bog Cycling
Bog Triathlon

# It Boggles the Mind

As with all sports, the best way to improve the game is to add a bike, especially if you're the sort who can't leave unwell enough alone. No surprise, then, that the creators of bog snorkeling introduced the annual World Mountain Bike Bog Snorkeling Championships to Llanwrtyd Wells in 2005. Talk about off-roading.

Competitors in mask and snorkel—eyes at water level—must, once again, ride two lengths of the bog. Their bikes are engineered with aerodynamic specifications opposite to those of what must be called—who knew?—"above-water cycling": Rather than light titanium, the frame of these bikes is composed of lead filled with water so riders don't float off. In 2008, Dan Bent rode in, pedaled through, and eventually emerged with victory, breaking the world record in just under a minute: 59.19 seconds.

Also making its debut in 2005, the Bog Triathlon, which challenges competitors to navigate a 7½-mile run, swim two lengths of the bog, and ride 19 miles on a mountain cycle. Dan Bent also holds this world record—2:23.14 hours—proving he sweats like a pig, loves mud like a pig, and rides a bike like Lance Armstrong dressed as a pig.

"**Competitors may stuff his or her pants with as much hay as possible.**"

—Robert Dover's Cotswold Olimpicks

It is said that in 1843, two men spent forty-five minutes battling in the streets of Manchester, wearing wooden clogs and kicking each other repeatedly in the legs. The crux of their difference? One pound. However much that would be in today's economy can't be enough to spend the better part of an hour offering one another what was colloquially known as "clog-toe pies" and "timber 'n' leather kisses."

Oh, and they were buck-naked. What that has to do with their conflict has been lost to history. What's not been lost: The winner of that battle later killed a man in a similar clog fight. This is not a sport for the faint of shin.

But after a century-long moratorium on competitive shin kicking, the brutal competition reemerged as an annual event in Great

Britain. Devoted participants are hoping to establish this distant step-brother of wrestling as an Olympic sport: "All we have to do is prove that Shin Kicking is played by men in 75 countries on four continents and women in 40 countries on three continents." So . . . all but done!

Nowadays, in hopes of maintaining a PG rating, competitors keep their clothes on. In fact, they stuff their pants with straw for protective cushioning, and wear sneakers rather than clogs or heavy boots. (Go on: Name one other sport where scarecrows would be considered worthy opponents.)

Arms straight, holding each other by the shoulders, opponents literally attempt to "kick the shin" out of each other, focusing on the tibia as they work to weaken each other's legs. The winner is he who, with one foot in the air, manages to throw his opponent to the ground. The first to fall loses, unless the referee declares an intentional trip or a kick above the knee, in which case the opponent wins the throw. Best two out of three throws moves onto the next round and is declared the winner, as long as "winner" can be defined as "he who gets to move onto the next round for more punishment and may or may not be able to stand on two feet come morning."

## Four More Things You Might Not Know About Shin Kicking

1. One of the original sports displayed at the Cotswold Olimpicks, shin kicking begun in 1612 by Robert Dover in tribute to, but with a cuter spelling of, the ancient Greek Olympics.
2. In the good-olden days, miners from Oldham, renowned for their shin-kicking prowess, were known for being as slippery as "snigs" or eels, as we would say today. Eventually, the cheaters were discovered lathering their bodies in soap before a match.
3. Because of the brutality (crippling injuries, wounded egos, soiled knickers), the sport all but died out by the 1900s. Yet something about the 1950s renewed the competition. Was it Elvis? That new-fangled device, the television? All that post-WWII free time?
4. Alcohol remains a steadfast tradition in the sport. (Okay, you might have guessed that.)

In the summer of 2012, the four hundredth Robert Dover's Cotswold Olimpick Games—featuring shin kicking, of course—will be played in Chipping Campden, during the very time that the Summer Olympic Games (merely the thirtieth) will be held in the somewhat larger venue of London.

"Fearlessness,
a fair amount
of agility, and a
high threshold
for pain."

—Vladimir Prochazka, Czech rock climber
and rock-climbing historian

Remember kids chanting, "Step on a crack . . . break your mother's back," as they jumped over gaps in the sidewalk?

In the sport of tower jumping, getting over the crack could mean breaking your own back or, more likely, your ankle. As for falling into the crack itself? That could mean swinging wildly into the face of a giant sandstone tower, hundreds of yards in the air. (A chant of "I want my mommy!" is more to the point.)

For those talented and/or intrepid enough to complete a death-defying leap across a rocky crevasse in a sport where "broken ribs and damaged spines are fairly common," the rewards must be pretty good. That probably depends on how "good" a free post-leap beer sounds. (The requisite pre-leap beers are full price.)

But for the locals of a northeastern Czech town near the Adrspach-Teplice rocks, "jumping is . . . for camaraderie and adrenaline," as one jumper stated. Apparently, entertainment options in the area have not hit rock bottom—just rock.

The Adrspach nature preserve is home to more than a thousand sandstone towers, many of which soar 300 feet into the air. Picture a ridge of half-size Washington Monuments. Since 1923, dozens of sandal-clad or barefoot athletes have practiced the art of leaping from tower to tower—a gap that's sometimes 10 or even 15 feet across—with only a knotted rope tied around the jumper's waist. (Traditional rock-climbing gear such as hooks, rings, cams, carabiners, or other metal, which can damage the fragile sandstone, are prohibited.) The last cord you needed this badly was umbilical.

In the 1960s, Petr Prachtel and his wife, Zorka—who often jumped without any rope, prudence, or soupcon of self-preservation—created a grading system to score a jump's difficulty. A Grade 1 jump can be "executed by any reasonably skilled climber." (Let's just forgo wondering what "reasonably" means here.) As the grades go higher, so does the difficulty level: By Grade 4, "the jump does not offer a flat landing surface, forcing the leaper to land monkey-style, clutching the crevices of the opposite wall." The first and only Grade 5 jump was executed by a man known only as Oxygen: He managed to land on the adjacent tower by grabbing hold of a single pine branch. Soon after his historic leap, which earned its own legendary name, "Amerika," Oxygen retired from tower jumping, moved to London, and became a gunsmith. It's all downhill once you're at the top.

> "Never do these children get so much attention as what they're getting now on top of these mattresses."
>
> —What's on When Web site

This Spanish "sport" ranks tenth among the world's dangerous festivals, according to AskMen.com, with their seven million monthly readers. Spain's Running of the Bulls takes first position, in which a chaos of runners tries to avoid being trampled or gored by bulls charging through the throngs of tourists that line the streets of Pamplona.

And yet, *this* sport is safe enough for babies. Well, probably not *American* babies. Here, athletically adept wunderkinds are harnessed by baby leashes, protected by 4-foot-high baby gates and cabinet latches even middle schoolers can't penetrate, dressed with baby helmets and kneepads (do they offer toddler roller hockey at Gymboree?), and outfitted with baby toupees to help them *acquire* their youthful good looks and allay any sign of Infantile Self-Image Anxiety.

But these precautions haven't made it to the Spanish village of Castrillo de Murcia, where, at their *El Salto del Colacho*, The Devil's Jump, parents lay their babies on embroidered pillows and a pristine white mattress of neatly pressed sheets in the middle of a narrow village street as some dude dressed in a yellow suit with red zig-zagging trim, brandishing a bludgeon and whip, laces up his PF Flyers and jumps, soaring just inches over the six to eight infants with their tiny waving arms and kicking feet. Not to worry, though: If *el colacho,* the guy who does

his best Carl-Lewis-in-a-devil-costume, successfully clears the babies, it is said that he rousts evil from their bodies and relieves them of original sin.

Before you start Googling for the Spanish equivalent of children's services, be aware that no baby has ever been injured during the four-hundred-year-old festival. Nonetheless, devils jumping over babies is not going to make its appearance at *your* local Gymboree center any time soon.

Do you have the government's AMBER Alert hotline on speed dial? Exorcise your fears at www.whatsonwhen.com. (Just put the festival name in the search box.)

# Leaps of Faith

Perhaps a leap between sandstone towers several stories in the air most resembles Robbie Knievel rocketing his motorcycle across 130 feet of air from one thirteen-story tower of timeshares in Las Vegas to the adjacent tower. But he did have a 200-foot ramp, a speed of 70 miles per hour, and more than just the thrust of a tower jumper's leg muscles to keep him from plummeting to the ground. For comparison, here are some other world-record leaps of faith.

Who: tower jumpers
Method: bare feet (or sandals) and a knotted rope
Distance: 10 to 15 feet
Notable Fact: They leap over fissures between sandstone towers, hundreds of feet in the air.

Who: Ray "The Human Frog" Ewry
Method: standing long jump
Distance: 11.38 feet
Notable Fact: The ten-time Olympic gold medal winner also holds the record for the standing high jump, leaping 5.41 feet into the air.

Who: Mike Powell
Method: running long jump
Distance: 29.36 feet
Notable Fact: Unlike tower jumpers, he can take twenty-plus strides before the big leap.

Who: Danny Way
Method: skateboard
Distance: 61 feet
Notable Fact: He just happened to jump the Great Wall of China.

Who: Dan Runte
Method: monster truck
Distance: 202 feet
Notable Fact: And he bounded over a grounded Boeing 727.

Who: Robbie Maddison
Method: motocross bike
Distance: 322 feet (The Aussie rider's goal was actually 360 feet.)
Notable Fact: That's more than the length of a football field.

Who: Robbie Knievel
Method: motorcycle
Distance: 24 Coke Zero delivery trucks
Notable Fact: This leap took place at Kings Island, a landlocked Ohio amusement park.

Who: Neil Armstrong
Method: spacesuit
Distance: 1 small step
Notable Fact: This "giant leap for mankind" took place July 21, 1969.

# six

## I Could Just Hurl . . .

To throw is human. (To catch, however, is canine.)

People throw things all the time. Say, we're happy: We toss the ball into the air after winning the semifinals. Say we're sad: We fling darts at an ex-girlfriend—at *a photo* of an ex-girlfriend. Say we're convinced there are no ashtrays left on Earth: We throw cigarette butts out the car window.

Babies throw tantrums. Brides throw bouquets. Boxers (or stood-up brides or really coordinated babies) throw left hooks.

We throw up, we throw down, we throw away, we overthrow—can it be any wonder that humans have thrown the very concept of throwing into the mix of sporting events?

In this chapter, you'll see a conglomeration of hurlers, heavers, pitchers, and flingers, filling the air with everything from a haggis to a human being, from a frozen tuna to what looks like a telephone pole.

And wherever these games are being held, you can hear the same primal shout: "Throw get 'em, tiger!"

They call it bowling, yet it has nothing to do with glossy white pins, oiled wooden lanes, or shoes, colorfully designed for humiliation, that have been worn by a dozen other strangers that day.

Some liken it to golf, but don't go looking for greens of gratuitously pampered grass and don't drag along those overly priced divot makers you call your set of clubs.

It says "road," and—well, actually, the sport *is* played on roads. Winding country roads with no "closed course" precautions taken to block tractors or delivery trucks from driving onto the playing course.

Irish road bowling has been played as early as the seventeenth century in Europe and no later than the Civil War in America. Indeed, Union and Confederate troops of Irish descent were said to have enjoyed the game with one another between battles. ('Tis true, 'tis true: Politics was more civilized centuries ago, when men could turn off hot buttons like succession and abolition for a few hours of intranational good sportsmanship and fun.) Today, Ireland hosts the annual European Bowling Championships, and three American Irish road bowling clubs, including the West Virginia Irish Road Bowling Association, host competitions as well. (Why road bowling caught on in "The Switzerland of the United States" is a true mystery; it's not as if John "Take me home, country roads" Denver was Irish!)

The goal of the competition is to see which individual or team can bowl an iron ball that's about the same circumference as a baseball—but five times the weight—across the finish line of a designated course in the fewest number of rolls. To bowl the "bullet," as it's called, players take a sprinting start up to the designated place in the road, a mark called the "butt." After the run, a player leaps in the air and releases the

bullet underhanded without going past the mark ("breaking his butt"), or merely damaging an adjacent spectator's knee.

The best players and teams generally designate someone to be the "road shower" (this has nothing to do with shampooing or conditioning the interstate). This is the person who stands ahead of the thrower to "show 'er or 'im" the best path for the bullet and who must be adept at what's known as "getting out of the way." Players then navigate their bullets along a 1- to 3-mile course, playing caroms off potholes, rummaging through curbside shrubbery to find their bullets, and even lofting the bullet into the air when faced with an especially tight turn in the course.

Most skilled players complete a course in twenty to twenty-five bowls. If two players cross the finish line in the same number of shots, the bowler whose bullet is farthest past the line wins—wins for himself, yes, but also for those who've bet thousands of euros on him, cheering, "*Faugh a ballach!*" That's Irish for "clear the way!"

There's a cannonball barreling toward your ankles right now at www.wvirishroadbowling.com or www.irishroadbowling.ie/about.htm.

"Snowballs, the sole weapon of the matches, are made with a specifically designed octopus dumpling–style snowball maker."

—Official yukigassen Web site

In *yukigassen,* Japan's organized sport of team snowball fighting, chilly artillery is thrown without fear of detention, lawsuit, or—we've all been there—sneering taunts of "You throw like a girl!" or "What's *that* jacket? Your sister's hand-me-down?" (Okay, so maybe "we all" just means us, in this case.)

Far from the playground or backyard, the Showa-Shinzan International Yukigassen tournament takes place at the base of a Japanese volcano. In front of 28,000 spectators, over 150 teams from around the world compete in a sport that requires "strong willpower, quick judgment, and intelligence"—as well as the self-confidence required to present a business card with the words PROFESSIONAL SNOWBALL FIGHTER.

Played seven against seven with an arsenal of ninety snowballs for each team, *yukigassen* is waged on a snow-covered, volleyball-sized court with three snow shields on each side and one in the middle. Each game comprises three periods; a team must win two of them to claim victory.

The teams, often dressed in wintry pirate regalia or *Baywatch* costumes, employ complicated strategies, as they . . .

- tag out opponents by hitting them with a sphere of frozen ammo
- hide behind one of the snow baffles to launch or avoid an icy orb of elimination
- perform their best imitation of James Bond (theme music reverberating in their ears) executing one of those spy rolls between two shields while simultaneously firing a flurry of glistening globes
- capture the opponents' flag, located in the middle of their side

Started in 1989 as a means to bolster winter tourism at the mountain (the "Come See the Volcano . . . Free Sno-cones for the Kiddies"

campaign went over like a lead snowball), the competition is now played at Mount Showa-Shinzan in Sobetsu, Japan, and at its sister cities in Finland and Norway. With various degrees of seriousness, the sport is also getting welcomed with anything but the cold shoulder in Canada, the United States, and other areas where winter means four months of gray skies, long nights, and seasonal affective disorder.

Each competition produces snowballs for each match in a standardized manner: Snow is heated to improve malleability, scooped

into a ninety-ball mold, and repeatedly packed into the mold until the snowballs are model-perfect and ready for action. (Would you expect less from a culture where apprentices study seven entire years to master the techniques of *gyodan,* the eighty-year-old art form of creating beautiful plastic replicas of food?)

Ready to start your own *yukigassen* league? Just remember, with 180 snowballs flying in a blizzard-like atmosphere, it can be difficult to tell friend from snow.

Looking for less "local color" than paintball?
Go snow-white at www.yukigassen.jp.

"Spectators are more than happy to have their faces smeared with mud."

—Samurai Dave

The Mudslinging Festival in Chiba, Japan, is one of many annual *hadaka* (Japanese for "naked") festivals. At the end of every February, thirty or so men donning white loincloths called *fundoshi* enter a frigid pond to engage in a mud-flinging free-for-all, soiling their man diapers as part of—what else?—a spiritual ritual.

Mud, known solely as the sworn enemy of carpets and kitchen floors in Western culture, represents good fortune and a bountiful harvest to the Japanese. To Westerners, it may also represent a curious form of parental care: Onlookers hand their infants to the mud-covered participants, who smear their muck on the babies' faces with a ceremonial stick.

Afterward, competitors warm themselves around a fire, before heading into the pond to engage in muddy mayhem. The battle begins as teams of human pyramids try to topple each other, but very quickly anarchy rules, with each man sludge-slinging for himself. Several times throughout the two-hour ordeal, the participants run back to the fire to regain a little sensation in their limbs, spreading luck by finger-painting spectators along the way.

Say what you like, but blessings of health and fortune come in many colors, guises, and textures, and who among us can afford to look askance at even a muddy one?

For eye-witness blogger Samurai Dave's full account, search "mudslinging" at www.samuraidave.wordpress.com.

When you conjure up images of civilization's first games, brawny
bronzed lads palming the discus . . . and oiled, muscular Adonises
clutching javelins come to mind. (Don't they? We're not alone here,
are we?) Throughout history, the ability to send an object farther
than anyone else has played a role in demonstrating who is the
dominant male entitled to breed with the females, and it's certainly
gentler on the body than butting heads like bighorn sheep or maul-
ing one another's flesh with tusks, like walruses.

Every culture must have its own unique arsenal of objects that
athletes or hotheaded chefs or coaches have sent flying. Yet none
appear to have perfected the art like the Scottish, whose Highland
Games always include:

**clatchneart:** a 16-pound "stone of strength," thrown like a shotput

**sheaf toss:** a burlap bale of hay that athletes attempt to fling with a pitchfork over the equivalent of a continually raised high-jump bar

**weight throw:** athletes spin a 28- or 56-pound weight attached to a cable around and around and toss it one-handed across the field

**hammer throw:** competitors whirl a 12-, 16-, or 22-pound ball at the end of a 4-foot cable above their heads and attempt to maintain balance, resist centrifugal force, and hurl the weight as far as possible

**caber toss:** athletes upend a humungous pole, run forward, and attempt to send it flipping forward into a perfect 12 o'clock landing

**bagpipe bands:** teams of pipers parade around at these events, causing spectators to consider the idea of how far they might be able to throw one of those caterwauling squeeze bags across the field

What follows is a hearty sampling of the world's favorite objects to hurl, from the truly hefty to the totally hare-brained.

# Haggis Hurling

*"The haggis must be of traditional construction: a tender boiled sheep's heart, lung and liver with spices, onions, suet and oatmeal and stock stuffed in a sheep's paunch, boiled for three hours."*

—Undiscovered Scotland: The Ultimate Online Guide

The rules also dictate that the haggis must be "packed tight and secure, with no extra 'skin' or 'flab,'" so that competitors, poised on a platform such as half a whiskey barrel, can toss Scotland's unofficial national dish as far as possible without the haggis bursting. If you're Alan Pettigrew you can throw a 1½-pound haggis, which most closely resembles a grapefruit-sized kidney stone, 180 feet 10 inches.

Controversy has surrounded the history of haggis hurling, as it was long believed that Scottish women in the seventeenth century brought a lunch of steaming haggis to toss across a wee stream to their laboring husbands. In 1977, Robin Dunseath wrote the definitive guide to the history and rules of the game, *The Complete Haggis Hurle.* And then, twenty-seven years later—was it scotch-induced remorse?—he admitted that the origins of the game were a definitive hoax.

And yet the game is not restricted to the gullible. Scotland sponsors the annual World Haggis Hurling Championships, and Sarnia, Ontario, plays host to the North American Haggis Hurling Championship, each fighting for the title of Most Necessary Waste of Food.

Hungry for more haggis? Hurl as much as you like at www.scottishhaggis.co.uk.

## Egg Throwing

"A sport enjoyed by millions of people since early humans discovered the delight of watching the failure of another to catch a tossed egg."

—World Egg Throwing Federation

You can't make an omelet—or an egg-throwing contest—without breaking eggs.

Now, an omelet is its own delicious reward. But when you're throwing an egg at another person, the big reward is hitting another's nether regions. (Nether regions, in this case, as in most others, means testicles.) Darrah Hardy, competing in the World Egg Throwing Championships' **accuracy competition,** apparently didn't realize she would receive the most points for targeting the nether regions of the renowned volunteer nicknamed Stupid Steve. (Pictured here, Steve describes himself as "a sandwich shy of a picnic.") Instead, the nine-year-old hit the man four consecutive times in the head—the second highest point-scoring spot—and managed to capture the title.

Competitors can't put all their eggs in one basket, however. Other disciplines at the competition, held annually in Lincolnshire, England, include the **egg-static relay,** in which eleven-player teams race to pass a dozen eggs, one by one, down a course, as well as the **trebuchet challenge,** where contestants build catapults to hurl eggs that must be caught by a teammate.

The **throwing and catching event** is fairly self-explanatory: Teammates begin about 33 feet apart (10 meters) tossing the egg; after each completed throw, they back up and throw again. In 1978, Texan Johnie Dell Foley successfully tossed an egg 323 feet 2 inches to his cousin Keith Thomas.

No telling, though, how Foley would have faired in the world championships' newest event, **egg Russian roulette.** Here, players are blindfolded and given six eggs: Five are hardboiled; one is raw. Competitors alternate smashing the eggs against their own heads. First to shoot themselves with a "yolking" gun loses. Still better than getting egged in the nether regions, right?

Still egging for more? See www.swatonvintageday.sslpowered.com/Champs.php.

# Going to Great Lengths

Here's the thrower's throne room, where the bosses of toss reign supreme. Moving from the far-flung to farthest flung, we have . . .

## Car Tire (your basic #35)
Hurler: Brian Oldfield, USA
Distance: 42 feet
Oldfield called AAA immediately afterward, realizing he had no spare.

## Paper Plate
Hurler: Alan Thomas, United Kingdom
Distance: 50 feet 8 inches
Luckily someone brought plenty of extras to the potluck.

## Shot Put
Hurler: Randy Barnes, USA
Distance: 75 feet 10¼ inches
Yes, this is the actual Olympic event. Considering the greater distances below, perhaps other objects also deserve a gold?

## Matchstick
Hurler: Uwe Hohn, Germany
Distance: 111 feet
It's another of those quit smoking tactics: Throw away your matches— throw them *really* far away!

## Frozen Tuna (whole)
Hurler: Sean Carlin, Australia
Distance: just under 122 feet 2 inches
Only spoiled fish are used at Tunarama, where $7,000 in prizes are awarded to spoiled people.

## Billiard Cue (not a billiard ball, but the stick)
Hurler: Dan Kornblum, Germany
Distance: 141 feet 4 inches
Seemingly impressive, but actually the world's longest scratch.

## Brick (standard 5-pound house brick)
Hurler: Dave Wattle, United Kingdom
Distance: 148 feet 6 inches
Nice, Dave, but why build that new garage as if you were observing a restraining order?

## Playing Card
Hurler: Rick Smith Jr., USA
Distance: 216 feet 4 inches
Smith, a magician, can actually slice bananas and watermelons with a thrown card. No matter what you're dealt, *let him win!*

## Frying Pan

Hurler: Jürgen Schult, Germany
Distance: just over 156 feet
   2 inches

You could hardly call Schult an *eine Eintagsfliege*. (That's German for "a flash in the pan"; can't blame us for frying.)

## Wellie/Gumboot (rubber boot)

Hurler: Jouni Viljanen, Finland
Distance: almost 214 feet
   4½ inches

Makes you wonder how far he could have flung it if someone were wearing the boot.

## Rolling Pin

Hurler: Lori La Deane Adams, USA
Distance: 175 feet 5 inches

She must not be the person in the family with the light touch when it comes to making pastry.

## Haggis

Hurler: Alan Pettigrew, England
Distance: 180 feet 10 inches

He's not only a heartbreaker but a heart thrower, too.

## Human Cannonball

Hurler: David "Cannonball"
   Smith Sr., USA
Distance: 185 feet 10 inches

He travels 70 miles per hour, although his voyage is only seconds long.

## Fruitcake (2 pound)

Hurler: Sean Hall, USA
Distance: 124 feet

After a heavy holiday meal, make this a new family tradition!

## Compact Disc

Hurler: Kim Flatow, Germany
Distance: 219 feet

Greater, but unofficial, distances are reported by people who've just spent ten minutes trying to open a shrink-wrapped CD.

## Cow Chip (1 pound)

Hurler: Steve Urner, USA
Distance: 266 feet

The athletes may shout "Chip ahoy!" before each toss.

## Cell Phone (battery included)

Hurler: Mikko Lampi, Finland
Distance: 311 feet 6 inches

The battery never held a charge, and Mikko never really liked the phone in the first place.

## Egg

Hurler: Johnie Dell Foley, USA
Distance: 323 feet 2 inches

No omelet for him, obviously.

## Baseball

Hurler: Glen Gorbous, Canada
Distance: 445 feet 10 inches

That's a record from 1957, set by a Canadian. So, baseball is *America's* great pastime?

Wood, in all of its many forms, is essential to human life. Fire, for instance, didn't just appear from a Zippo lighter. Wood—a lot of wood—was vital in the building of Noah's Ark (as was Home Depot, which biblical scholars continue to censure). A little "wooden" can describe that previous bit of humor. "Wood" paneling adorned many station wagons in the late twentieth century. So is it any surprise that wood has pervaded the world of sports? (Probably not, if we're including it in this book.)

## Caber Toss

"It took me five games before
I turned my first caber."
—Professional Highland Games thrower Daniel McKim

Chopping lumber isn't for everyone. Perhaps it's the stereotype of tacky plaid shirts and itchy, saw-dusted beards.

But those looking to out-tacky even a lumberjack get-up will slip on their kilts and have a go at tossing the caber. Said to have evolved from foresters throwing tree trunks into a river, this sport of heaving a giant wooden pole is practiced at Scottish Highland Games globally. There's no standard height or weight for the caber, although most range between 16 and 20 feet, and 80 and 130 pounds. The largest ever recorded in competition tipped the scales, and the competitors, at a daunting 25 feet and 280 pounds.

A caber toss occurs in several steps. First, assistants lift the small end of the caber into the air until the thrower can balance it by himself, while the large end rests on the ground. The thrower then works his hands toward the bottom of the caber, lifting it from the ground until it rests against his chest and shoulder. After a short run, the caber begins leaning off the thrower's chest, and he releases the caber from his midsection: The brute strength and phallic image are obvious to all.

While some American competitions measure the distance of the throw, success is generally based on how straight the toss is. That is, the thrower's goal is to have the caber land perfectly straight away from his body. Based on the hour hand of a clock, a perfect toss is called "a 12 o'clock"—otherwise known as time for an Old Chub ale and a serving of haggis (page 147).

## Basque Wood Chopping (*Aizkolaris*)

"Tradition has it, that the prize is a herd of rams."
—*World Sports Encyclopedia*

Okay, fine: It's not *wood*—it's *timber*. Whatever it's called, some folks just aren't satisfied by the fact that it's no longer a growing tree. So they cut it up more—for money. Or, in the case of the hundred-year-old Basque wood-chopping competition known as *aizkolaris*, they compete for a herd of rams.

The sport is said to date back to medieval times and was recorded beginning in the nineteenth century. Today, at the *Urrezko Aizkora* ("Golden Axe"), held in Spain's Basque country, they award cash prizes, not to mention pride and a possible sponsorship endorsement with Elmer's Interior Wood Glue. An *aizkolaris* is a staple of Basque festivals, many of which have seen up to thirty thousand spectators, radio and TV broadcasts, and ax-wielders from as far away as Australia and the United States. A competitor stands horizontally across a chunk of tree trunk, chopping down the middle until the lumber between his ankles is severed. It's speed, not points, that wins this event; chopping between your own two feet seems to be enough incentive for precision.

Many of today's ax-wielding events around the world, such as the Lumberjack World Championships in Hayward, Wisconsin, and the STIHL Timbersports World Championships in Farmley, Ireland, use logs with a 12- or 16-inch diameter: Those contests are over in a matter of seconds. But the logs used in the *aizkolaris* events have a minimum diameter of 36 inches, often range between 45 and 60 inches, and sometimes include logs over 100 inches across in a bonus round: These competitions last significantly longer, and choppers generally whittle away at anywhere between six and twenty logs, which can require hours of nerve-wracking whacking and hacking. In 1924, a man completed twenty 54-inch trunks in 1:09:32, earning him a herd of well-deserved rams and the record for world's largest "paper cut."

# The Wide Wood of Sports

Still lumbering around, wondering what timbering sports can offer you? Not even counting events with crosscut saws, chainsaws, hatchets, or Pick-up Sticks, you might consider these options:

**boom run:** Here competitors try to have the fastest time crossing a course of logs (or "booms") floating end to end in a body of water.

**logrolling** or **birling:** Two competitors stand on a single floating log and use their feet to spin it, attempting to force their opponent to lose balance and dump into the water.

**90-foot speed climb:** Wearing spurred shoes, athletes climb ropes to scale a 90-foot cedar pole and slide back down as quickly as possible. Oregon's Brian Bartow holds the world record with a time of 19.87 seconds.

**springboard chopping:** Competitors cut into the side of a 9-foot pole until they can insert a wooden platform, called a springboard. Climbing onto the springboard, they chop another slot to insert another springboard. And so on, and so on, until they reach the top of the pole and chop a 12-inch-diameter log mounted to the top. This is old-time logging at its very best! Dave Bolstad's time of 41.15 seconds set the world record in 2003. Is it a wonder deforestation plagues the biosphere?

> **"Most fierljeppers wear rubber bicycle inner tubes around their ankles. This, along with sticky spray, gives a good grip on the pole."**

—Polsstokbond Holland

Many kids may *consider* climbing to the top of a telephone pole or a flagpole, but few see these daft and risky dreams through . . . beyond shimmying a few feet into the air, or sticking a tentative tongue on an icy pole as a wintertime whim.

Spring and summer in the Netherlands present a different story, where climbers scale poles—originally wooden ones—*not* to retrieve some camper's underpants sling-shot to the top, but for Dutch supremacy. Yep, it's *fierljeppen*, West Frisian for "far leaping," a sport in which athletes hurl their own bodies . . . up, out, and over.

A pole as long as 43 feet 6 inches is anchored in a canal and leans toward a dock. A competitor takes a quick sprint across the runway and dock, leaps to grab the pole, and hurriedly climbs to the top as the pole leans forward across the almost forty-foot-deep pond, before bounding into the sand pit on the other side of the canal. The *fierljepper* who travels the farthest wins. Think running pole-vault start, rope-climb middle, and long-jump landing.

First recorded as early as 1200, the idea of *fierljeppen* was created by farmers when they used large poles to cross waterways that divided plots of land. Some say that poachers developed this technique to steal eggs from farmers, vaulting over and back before a *Hollandse Herdershond* (Dutch Shepherd dog) bit them in the *achterwerk* (behind). Even

before this, some say that Moses didn't part the Red Sea so much as use his staff to vault across it. (Yes, Moses was also involved with stone skipping. *That's* why he's so famous!)

Reliable records about the sport date from 1771, and today, competitions remain popular among the Dutch and the Germanic peoples of the Dutch province of Friesland. (Oddly, "Friesland" doesn't translate as "land of fries," although *patat*—fried lengths of potato typically served with mayonnaise—is a popular local dish.)

In 1957, competitions began in Friesland; the Dutch held a similar competition in 1960. Six years later, the first match between the two regions was held. Currently, Frisian Bart Helmholt holds the world record with a jump of over 68 feet (20.76 meters). That's long enough to clear an eighteen-wheeler with room to spare.

While the English-speaking world remains unclear about how to translate *fierljeppen*—pole leaping? canal jumping? ditch vaulting?—it seems clear on what to call *fierljeppers* who land in the water: Soggy Fries.

Always wanted to slide down poles like a firefighter? Take the *real* challenge, and climb up to www.pbholland.com/?&lang=en.

"The slower the pole goes to the other side, the more time you have to climb to the top. If you don't have enough speed . . . you fall in the water. If the pole doesn't go straight to the other side, you lose distance. Climbing is the easy part."

—Pieter Hielema, veteran *fierljepper*

## What Runs Through a Fierljepper's Mind Before a Jump

Okay, concentrate. Concentrate. I can do this. *But if . . .*

I run too fast or too slow . . . *I won't be able to . . .*

leap from the dock at the right point in my stride . . . *and I won't be able to . . .*

jump exactly straight at the pole so that my legs catch on both sides and I can pull myself onto the pole . . . *so I won't be able to . . .*

climb all the way to the top before the pole swings over to the sand pit . . . *and I won't be able to . . .*

kick my legs up parallel to the pole and push off to get that extra 3 meters on the landing . . . *which means I'll be landing in the water again.*

Yeah, well, it's not that cold today.

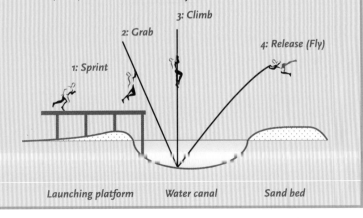

*1: Sprint*  *2: Grab*  *3: Climb*  *4: Release (Fly)*

*Launching platform*  *Water canal*  *Sand bed*

# seven

# Wrong Place,
# Wrong Time

Fair play must certainly be the first Golden Rule of Sports. Gathered here are competitions that break a few *other* golden rules, such as "Never put things where they don't belong." But unlike sticking a finger in an electrical socket, placing tinfoil in the microwave, or losing your wedding ring while cleaning the bottom of your goldfish pond, these misplaced games won't leave you fried, smoked, or in deep shit (well, except maybe in a game of elephant polo).

These outlandish sportsters are so far out of bounds that they've taken even the most common and popular of games, soccer, and subjected competitors to the unique hazards of kicking and slide-tackling in swamps or snowdrifts. Unicycling fanatics, not content with merely not falling off, take their wheel to terrains reserved for basketballs, hockey pucks, and mountain bikes.

Here are new subspecies of sports—mutants that are evolving to fill some curious emptiness in the phys ed biosphere.

Leagues are already starting in a neighborhood near you.

"The only
thing between
you and
scoring . . .
is the need
to breathe."

—Underwater Society of America

What if, during an ice hockey game, the surface melted, and all the players sunk to the bottom of what turned out to be a swimming pool, and then continued the game? You'd have Octopush, a sport that has gone over—or gone *under*—in a dozen countries world-wide, including the United States, where you thought only leaping killer whales or Michael Phelps could fill a natatorium.

Underwater hockey was created in 1954 under the name "Octopush" by British SCUBA divers looking to stay in shape during the winter months. While the founders are apparently opposed to calling it "underwater hockey" because "the game was created independent of any land-based game," you can call it what you like: With a snorkel in your mouth, no one can understand you anyway. Besides, the rules are always the same: Two six-player teams (no goalie), equipped with a 1-foot stick (originally called a "pusher"), fins, mask, snorkel, and a protective glove, attempt to score a 3-pound puck, also known as the "squid," into the opposing team's goal. (And as this book's title states, players must slide the squid along the bottom of the pool: No dribbling of the squid is permitted.)

The "supreme anaerobic game" is literally breathtaking: Players bob up and down, judging when to breathe, before diving back down to the pool's bottom, where the entire game takes place. The best players "can drop from the surface to steal the puck from an unsuspecting opponent or take a pass from a teammate to score." Unlike hockey players, who need to be burly (a helmet and skates add at least 10 pounds), for underwater players "the water nullifies pure mass advantage and emphasizes clever use of torque." This often gives women, smaller players, and competitors who know what "torque" means the clear advantage.

More good news for these smaller swimmers: The sport is supposed to be noncontact. But similar to ice hockey, here the inevitable injuries include an occasional blackout from overexertion, broken noses or teeth from an elbow or fin slap, and most commonly, cuts on the knuckles and knees from scraping the pool bottom.

Deep breath . . . hold . . . come up for air at www.usauwh.com.

"[Players] will come down on top of you, kind of like a giant submarine, and smash you," says Jonny O'Brion, a University of Illinois player. "I've had that happen a few times."

# Underwater Olympics

The modern Olympic Games, despite being played for the past 113 years, attracting sixteen thousand athletes from 205 countries, and charging an average of $750,000 for a thirty-second television commercial, have finally sunk to new depths.

As if China didn't have enough publicity for the 2008 Summer Olympic Games (even the astronauts could see that advertisement on the Great Wall!), the city of Qingdao hosted the Underwater Olympic Games in 2008 to hype the Beijing Games.

At Qingdao's Underwater World aquarium, submerged competitions included relay races, underwater weight-lifting, and Olympic standards like:

**fencing:** No gambling necessary to bribe one competitor to "take a dive."
**shooting:** Proficiency in this sport can be useful, as proven by *Jaws*.
**gymnastics:** Like we all can't do a handstand in the water? Sheesh.
**basketball:** [Your turn! Insert the "dunk" joke of your choice here.]

The divers, who trained for over a year and a half for these competitions, faced unique challenges performing their sports in water: increased breath control, building strength to deal with water resistance, balancing or landing difficulties due to buoyancy. They also got really pruney skin.

For shooting and fencing events, athletes were required to balance on a wire, wear a heavy air tank on their backs, and try to maintain some kind of aim in the water's denser atmosphere.

"Although it's cold and toilsome," one athlete admitted, "we still love our work . . . and hope our performance will bring more fun and fresh experiences to our visitors."

*Fresh* indeed. You didn't expect all this fun in saltwater, did you?

"The football may not be carried in a player's bathing suit or any other article of clothing."

—Underwater Football rule book

While the syringe has adversely affected many sports nowadays—congressional hearings on baseball!—it's vital to your neighborhood game of underwater football. Who would've thought? (It also helps to be dating a nurse or a vet tech.)

To make the ball sink, you take the air out of a child-size basketball or normal football and then give it several injections of corn syrup. Once full, the ball is sanded to give it better hydrodynamics for the business of aquatic horseplay. To score a goal, a team must carry and pass the ball across the pool while completely submerged. When a player has the ball, no part of his body may be above the surface—except in an act of scoring, which involves smacking the ball on the pool deck at the opponent's end.

Created in the 1960s by a Manitoba SCUBA instructor (clearly, these folks had a lot of time between dives), underwater football is played throughout Canada. Curiously, despite Canada's noncombative mind-set, tackling the ball-carrier is legal; physicality in the game is encouraged, so injuries do occur. Athletes admit that one of the best ways to burst an eardrum is to be whacked by a flipper.

With Canadian safety-first mentality in mind, the Web site cautions: "If you are not comfortable in the water or you do not know how to swim, you should consider taking swimming lessons before you join the fun." Or stick to playing the old boring land version of the game.

## Underwater Cycling

In 1983, while leading a dive for German tourists, Italian cyclist and diver Vittorio Innocente found an old bicycle on the seabed and began riding it, inadvertently creating a new sport: underwater cycling.

In 2008, seven years after he broke the speed record for underwater cycling (¾ mile in a swimming pool at a blazing average speed of nearly 2 miles per hour—talk about setting the water on fire!—Innocente attempted to break the distance record. And while he had no concerns about oiling his bike chain or catching his pant legs in it, Innocente had plenty to worry about:

- going down 92 feet into the Mediterranean Sea
- staying down (the bike had to be weighted with 77 pounds of ballast and equipped with water-logged tires, fins, and spoilers)
- being sixty-two years old
- encountering the rugged, rocky, muddy terrain of the underwater slope

And yet, pedaling 213 feet in nine minutes, Innocente broke his previous record of 197 feet. Didn't even break a sweat—although who can tell underwater?

## Turf 'n' Surf

Anyone with a working knowledge of American history knows that surfing was created by a 1960s West Coast rock band to provide the group with a subject for its lyrics.

Those who were turned off by the Beach Boys' falsetto harmonies, who couldn't get the keys to Daddy's "fun, fun, fun" T-Bird, and who never managed to shack up with a real "California girl" must be responsible for inventing surfing's antithesis, snowboarding, where bodies, swaddled in sleeping bag–size outfits, ride the "tide" of a snow-covered slope.

*Wouldn't it be nice,* boarding enthusiasts later thought to themselves, *if we freed our sport from the tyrannical limitations of Nature?* Their answer—a "yes" in three-part harmony—begat two new surfing styles, even though "Skimboarding USA" and "Sandboarder Girl" don't quite have the same Top 40 ring.

## Skimboarding

Moving in the wrong direction generally ends badly: being ridiculed for starting the salad bar at the dressing end; for remembering, three steps up, that you need to take the *down* escalator; realizing that you're working the Bob Evans place mat maze from the wrong end as you see your six-year-old niece has already helped Biscuit find Gravy.

Want to right those wrongs? Take up skimboarding, in which moving the wrong way is the only way.

Unlike surfers, skimmers start on the beach. As a wave approaches,

they run toward the water, slam the board down, and hydroplane across the thick water from the crashing wave or the thin layer of water from a receding wave. Once in the water, a skimmer might ride "down the line," horizontally across the beach, or head straight into the water, launching into an aerial trick over the wave.

The 1920s in Laguna Beach, California, saw the makings of skimboarding, as lifeguards were seen riding pieces of plywood into the water while sharks and undertows swallowed tourists in the blink of an eye (or several blinks, if you got sand in yours). Since the Roaring '20s ("roaring" for the cries of skimmers with splinters in their feet), the skimboard has evolved into a fiberglass vehicle, about half the length of a surfboard, prompting some to say the sport is "like sliding a tray down the rails of the cafeteria line."

While California remains its center, the United Skim Tour—slightly less fattening than the United Two-percent or United Whole Tour—hosts competitions on America's East Coast, Europe, and South America. But the tour's biggest stop is Aliso Beach Park in Laguna for the Victoria Skimboards World Championship of Skimboarding, which, in its thirty-third year in 2000, attracts the world's sixty best professionals, eighty best amateurs, and the most subjective judges. How does a competitor impress these judges? Of course, riding down the line for as long as possible and pulling aerials and 360s don't hurt, but according to the officials, "The truth is that there is no criteria."

Tired of just surfing the Web? Try skimming at www.skimonline.com.

# Sandboarding

Just as some people like to talk about infinity in terms of snowflakes—no two are alike—others describe it in grittier terms: It's like grains of sand on the beach. Can it be a coincidence that both particles are ideal for boarding? Yeah, probably.

In regions where snow's unlikely to provide much of a surfing surface, athletes go sandboarding. First seen in California in the 1980s, barefooted pilots ride waxed-up snowboards down steep sand dunes at speeds of over 50 miles per hour. Boarding on dunes in Europe, Egypt, and the Middle East has people spending as much time in the sand as golfers afflicted with a bad slice.

While the difficulty of building a ski lift on sand dunes does delimit the sport's popularity, as well as the chance to come home with lift tags pinned to your windbreaker, complexes such as Oregon's Sand Master Park are attempting to change this, providing equipment rentals, lessons, and 42 acres of sand mountains.

Monte Kaolino in Hirschau, Germany, plays host to the Sandboarding World Championships, at which competitors vie for international supremacy and first dibs at that mirage of a soda machine. The contests include:

In the **sandboardercross** event, pilots deftly navigate slaloms and race through tight turns.

**Sand slopestyle** competitions feature flips and spins off large ramps; professional Josh Tenge holds the Guinness World Record for the longest distance sandboard backflip: 44 feet 10 inches.

And in the **sand waterslide** competition, boarders attempt to ride into a small pond and skim across the water's surface—a contest that leaves much less sand in the competitors' shorts.

The only *genuine* trick every competitor faces: how to convince the airlines not to charge extra for bringing along a skimboard. (Alas, it will not fit in the overhead compartment.)

Want to add a little grit to your sporting diet? See www.sandboard.com.

### Dirt Boaters and Ice Sailors

The majority of us don't know more than the basic definition of a sailboat—"a hole in the water through which you pour money"—offered up by owners of the crafts. What's a "halyard" or a "boom vang" or a "scupper"? Is "daggerboard" a game of pirate darts? Is "turtling" when you're caught in a lap lane behind a cardiac-rehab "swimmer"? And you need a "forward pulpit" for . . . what—beseeching the wind gods?

But most of us *would* go out on a limb or a dock and confidently say that sailboats belong in water, sort of the way toddlers in restaurants belong in their booster seats and not three or four tables away from Mommy, amusing the one doting person at your table. And yet the very vitality of a sport requires evolution. In the case of sailing, zealous landlubbers have brought the idea of wind-propelled boating squarely onto terra firma: specifically, onto the sandy beaches of New Zealand and the frozen lakes of Sweden.

But perhaps these sports can offer renewed honesty to all those beachless, lakeless, landlocked motels and high-rises with names like "Watercourse," "Oceanview," and "Sea Breeze."

## Land Sailing

*"All you need to know is whether it's windy or not."*
—Blokart's official Web site

Nobody likes an oxymoron. Low-sodium bacon? Working vacation? Hollywood marriage? Athlete scholar? In this sense, land sailing—despite having eight size and shape classes (not to mention a record speed of 116.7 miles per hour)—can't compete with its easily assembled, inexpensive, and cleverly named brethren, blokarts, "the best toys on the planet." (Pronounce it "blow cart," and the name makes some sense.)

This wind-powered vehicle, invented by New Zealand's Paul Beckett, sails across the sand powered solely by wind. Three wheels support the cockpit, which is attached to the sail, and the driver steers with one hand and pulls the sail's sheet with the other. The easy-to-assemble-and-maneuver kart, weighing all of 65 pounds and transported in a bag (matching shoes, optional), is often seen careening about parking lots, beaches, and tennis courts from South Africa to Lithuania, from South Beach to Japan (not the same vehicle, of course).

The International Blokart Racing Association holds competitions around the globe, including the Kellogg's Nutri-Grain World Blokart Championships in New Zealand. Karting for fun, drivers may balance on two wheels or pull 360-degree turns; during races, however, blokarts

reach top speeds of nearly 55 miles per hour. Race officials point out that the slowest recorded speed of a blokart is zero miles per hour, in which case the vehicle could be called a slokart. And that, as we know, is an oxymoron, which no one likes.

Do you have two arms and weigh less than 265 pounds? You fit the blokart criteria! Check out www.blokart.com.

## Ice Yachting

"Racing by to the singing of the wind in your rigging and the crisp cutting sound of the sharp-bladed runners."
—*Time*

Thought that ice sculpture of the *Santa Maria* in the punch fountain at the club's Christmas party was pretty swell, huh? Turns out ice boats are even more impressive when, mounted on skates, they're speeding across a frozen lake at 60 miles per hour. Now we're talking *punch!*

Poughkeepsie, New York, organized America's first Ice Yachting Club in 1861. Then, in 1936, the *Detroit News* got in on the action and sponsored a competition for the design of the fastest ice boat; the winning entry, known ever after as the DN, went into production; it's now the largest and most popular class of ice boats in the world. Currently, over two thousand sailors have a membership in the International DN Ice Yacht Racing Association (half in North America, the other half in Europe), representing twenty nations worldwide. They compete in the class's own world championships, the oh-so-original sounding Gold Cup, which has been held every year since 1973, along with Gold Cups in hockey, soccer, horse racing, sailfish tournaments, and umpteen other sports that think "gold" and "cup" are the recipe for the biggest win.

Up to sixty DN boats (12 feet in length and weighing between 100 and 150 pounds) race five laps around a triangle with 1-mile-long legs. While these yachts could keep up on a freeway, the world tries to keep pace with Norway and Sweden: The Stockholm Ice Yacht Club has the largest active ice boat fleet in the world.

According to the IDNIYRA, the essential conditions for ice sailing are fairly obvious: "access to a lake (or sea bay)," "at least 6-inch-thick ice," "wind," and "minimal snow." Oh yeah, and one of these boats.

Sail the seven frozen seas at www.idniyra.org.

## Set Sail

Landlocked? Icebound? Lovelorn? Clueless? Whatever? Choose your ideal sea-unworthy adventure with help from the chart below.

| Tie-breaking Question | DN Ice-yachting Boats | Blokart Sand-sailing Boats |
|---|---|---|
| So how big's the sail? | It's 60 square feet; a bit smaller than an 8x8-foot banquet tablecloth. | They come in 3-, 4-, or 5.5-meter sails (bigger sail=faster speed). |
| How tall's that mast? | Sixteen feet— coincidentally, that's the name of the Swathmore College all-male a cappella group. | Fully assembled, it stands 13 feet 9 inches. |
| How many can ride at once? | You and two friends (one front steering runner, two side runners). | Just you, or just your friend—whoever coughed up the $2,500 for the entry-level blokart. |
| What happens if you tip over? | Just a little sliding on the ice, nothing like that triple toe loop. | With the sail on the ground, you're grounded, too. |
| I'm concerned about the environment! What impact will this have? | None. Wind's the only fuel, so chill out and enjoy the chill! | None. Once again, wind is renewable. It's just not as predictable as gasoline. |

| Tie-breaking Question | DN Ice-yachting Boats | Blokart Sand-sailing Boats |
|---|---|---|
| Does the craft come with any nifty features? | A discount subscription to the *Detroit News* would be nice, but no. | Seat belts, the very zenith of nifty features, which are required. |
| How heavy is this thing, if I'm going to have to lug it clear across tarnation and back? | A mere 100–150 pounds. (That does not include your "galley kitchen" cooler of beers.) | Just 55–65 pounds— about as much as an overstuffed suitcase you hope the airline doesn't weigh at check-in. |
| Can I also sail it on the water? | Sure, as long as the water is in its frozen state. | Only long enough for you to climb aboard. |
| Can the whole shebang fit in my car trunk, if I clean it out? | Not happening. And not just because you're only *saying* that you'll clean out your trunk. | That's the beauty of this beast; it packs into a bag that's just over 3¾ feet long. |
| What other supplies do I need onboard? | Lip balm, winter clothing, Little Hotties Hand, Pocket & Glove Warmers. | 30 SPF sunscreen, beverages—if only the Hotties folks made something equivalent . . . like Long Cool Shower in a Sack. |
| What do most people do after a day's sailing? | Pray for spring. | Bury losers up to their chins in sand. |

## What's the Best Brand of Soccer?
## Take Your Kick.

The perfectly natural action of kicking a round object across a flat surface has origins in many countries and your choice of the past three millennia.

Today, with more fans than basketball, baseball, and football all jammed together in one theoretical stadium, soccer boasts billions of players and spectators around the globe. Over twenty-seven days, an estimated 33 billion viewers watched the 1998 FIFA World Cup. (Perhaps the 2010 games, to be hosted in South Africa, will eclipse even those numbers.) After spending nearly a month in front of the television, those soccer-saturated viewers practically *had* to get off their butts. Perhaps that's how FIFA-fans spun off these *IFFY* soccer variations:

**beach soccer:** Popular for many years, this version features a playing field of sand that makes cooling off in the ocean *almost* as attractive as the Brazilian notion of a topless game.

**criss-cross soccer:** Here, two games of soccer with four teams are played simultaneously on two fields, which intersect in the middle. Kind of like a game of Chinese checkers, but with concussions.

**blind soccer:** Argentina hosts the Blind World Cup, a five-on-five tournament in which blindfolded players (plus a sighted goalie) are guided around the field by voice commands of a sighted partner to locate a ball that contains small pieces of metal so players can hear it.

**RoboCup Project:** This is an international project that hopes, by 2050, to "develop a team of fully autonomous humanoid robots that can win against the human world champion team in soccer." While the designers are cobbling together "autonomous agents, multi-agent collaboration, strategy acquisition, real-time reasoning, robotics, and sensor-fusion" to create their 'bots, the rest of us will be watching Cristiano Ronaldo's *son* kicking serious human butt on the field.

In addition to these four, three other soccer satellite games should be on your radar.

## Rollersoccer

"To promote the sport, Zack incessantly kicked his soccer ball towards . . . random skaters everywhere he went."
—Zack "Soccerhead" Phillips's Web site

Safety is key in this game, and we don't mean just remembering to leave your valuables at home before practice. Players strap on helmets. They wear shin guards. They may even use drops to prevent ear infections, since keeping your equilibrium "inline" is a must in rollersoccer.

In 1995, Zack "Soccerhead" Phillips started this soccer-on-skates game in San Francisco. The game is played five versus five on a standard roller rink; it's one point for a goal, and two if the ball passes through a defender's legs on the way to the goal. There are no hands, no designated goalies, and no way *watching* roller derby will prepare you to play in the annual Rollersoccer World Cup, which, held since 2002, crowned the United States as champion in 2008.

A game that's gained international popularity with its "ultrafast tempo" and quick turnovers, rollersoccer involves the skills of several sports. Players master different types of kicks:

**side kick:** Using the inside of the foot, a kicker can deliver accuracy and control.

**toe kick:** The tip of the skate offers maximum power when shooting.

**instep kick:** Making contact with the top outside of his foot, a player gets both power and accuracy with this most difficult shot.

The Rollersoccer International Federation says that despite the occasional face-plant, playing rollersoccer is one of the best ways to improve your inline skating. "Since the objective is the ball and your means are the wheels, your body learns to skate without your brain (anxiety, fear) getting in the way." *Brainless*—just as they say.

In 1996, rollersoccer's creator decided to cut his hair into quite the "ballsy" 'do. With narrow lines of hair connecting pentagonal patches of hair, Zack's 'do perfectly resembled a soccer ball. After years of self-styling to maintain the cut, Zack finally had the pattern tattooed onto his scalp. Talk about keeping your head in the game.

"Got balls?" as the site's welcome screen asks. Prove it at www.rollersoccer.com.

# Swamp Soccer

For centuries, no one complained about a lack of balls in mud wrestling. Recently, however, Finnish cross-country skiers, during summer training in swamps, added one to the mix and made up swamp soccer, like their very own mud pie.

Though many are the fans of soccer, few relish the idea of yellow fever, so this game isn't played in an actual swamp but rather on a dirt field supersaturated with water. While basic soccer rules apply—except for the fact that corner kicks, free kicks, and penalty kicks are taken by punting—players must adhere to a strict uniform code. "Players on each team should wear the same color tops. Fancy dress is allowed," the rule book reads. To some men, this means skirts and tube tops; to selected women, full tuxedos. Another uniform rule: Players aren't allowed to change their shoes during the game.

While mud wrestling may still win a popularity contest among guys, Finland's first thirteen-team swamp soccer tournament has grown into an annual competition with over 250 teams, and every play is a dirty one.

# Snow Soccer (*Umpihankifutis*)

*"Some people try to use an actual snow soccer ball—made of snow—but that doesn't work too well."*
—From www.suopotkupallo.fi

There are many ways to injure yourself in the snow. There's frostbite. There's the possibility of slipping and falling: A quarter-inch of snow, despite the looks of it, doesn't leave much room between you and con-

crete; and deeper snow, despite appearing like a fresh mound of powder to jump in, can conceal an otherwise conspicuous fire hydrant.

With the advent of snow soccer, there's now another option: being smacked by a frozen-hard soccer ball on your frigid-fleshed thigh.

Perhaps it seems logical (at least to the Finnish) that this sport grew out of the success of their swamp soccer; apparently *brrr!* is their new *yuck!* In 2006, Finland held a World Cup competition, and Tomsk, Siberia, now hosts its annual tournament, the Siberian Snow Ball.

In heavy boots and padded snow pants, the teams surely have the greatest difficulty with running back and forth in thick snow. What's the only thing that could possibly make this form of soccer *more* challenging? Perhaps the athletes' mothers on the sidelines, nagging the players to zip up their coats?

"There's just something satisfying about taking an inherently unstable vehicle like a unicycle, and riding it places nobody thought it could go."

—www.unicyling.com

## Reinventing the Wheel

Riding a unicycle presents a host of dangers even besides the obvious fact that things are *missing*: the other wheel, handlebars, brakes, a kickstand, a horn or bell, a headlight, reflectors, a little basket to carry your parcels from the farmers' market! Plus, there's the problem of trying to see around your bulbous scarlet nose in order to dodge the dressed-up elephants and white-faced guys on stilts. And there's the potential hazard of keeping your size 26 shoes out of the spokes while juggling your flaming rings.

Playing polo on a unicycle, however, is hardly a matter of clowning around.

And yet, according to at least one athlete from Oregon, it's "pretty easy." Then, holding up his cast, he added, "I busted my arm

on Monday, but that's my fault for not wearing body armor."

While polo is but one of many entertaining unicycle competitions, uni sports—tennis, hockey, basketball, climbing mountains, and so forth—are anything but a circus.

Imagine all the most hazardous and rugged terrains an auto company might use to film its new 4x4 truck commercial. You there? Now go and grab your unicycle out of the truck bed, hop on, and start pedaling. This is mountain unicycling, commonly called MUni (as in Mountain Unicycle) by those uncommonly fearless folks with an unmatched sense of equilibrium and an unequaled lack of common sense.

MUni riders take their one-wheeled wonders through forests, across rocky topography, into creeks, along ledges, on ice, and over 6-foot drops by taking on the "awesome challenge of mastering the skills to maneuver, balance, and react . . . over difficult terrain." At the International Unicycling Federation's Unicycling Convention and Championships (New Zealand hosts the fifteenth edition of the biannual UNICON in 2009), riders compete in an uphill race, a 1½-mile downhill race, and a cross-country race through at least 3 miles of off-road course.

Riders train themselves to navigate bumps and curbs, ride backward, and hop, either to regain balance, hurdle obstacles, or pull off 360 degree uni spins. No worries, though, "safety"—according to unicycling Web host John Foss—is the first rule of MUni.

The second rule ought to be: "Go home right now and get a *second* wheel."

Feeling MUni-ficent? Try www.unicycling.com.

# Reeling and Wheeling

Contrary to popular belief, this sport is far from uni-dimensional. At the UNI-CON World Championships, unicyclists compete in a variety of races, including hockey, sprints, and even a unicycle marathon (well, 42 kilometers is marathon enough for balancing on that seat). Check out these other innovative one-wheeled wonder-whys:

**standard skill:** Riding on an 11x14-meter lane, participants are awarded for the creativity, difficulty, and execution of up to eighteen performed tricks, including riding with the seat dragging on the floor, coasting while standing up, and executing 740-degree spins.

**slow race:** Riding across a board that's 10 meters long (and only 6 inches wide for competitors older than eleven), a unicyclist must cycle as slowly as possible without stopping. The winner in 2008 took nearly 1 minute 11 seconds.

**wheel walk:** In this race, participants propel the unicycle not by pedaling but instead by pushing the tire with their feet.

**basketball:** In unicycle basketball, a player must stay mounted at all times, except to dunk the ball (okay, so the hoops are lowered) or block a shot. The rules state: "The player is allowed two steps. A step is a half revolution of the wheel, meaning that each wheel revolution is the equivalent of two steps because pedaling with one leg only moves the wheel half a revolution."

**freestyle:** There are individual, pair, and group competitions here, in which competitors perform to music, with an emphasis on creativity, use of props, and variety of skills. Props: Always a questionable addition to a sport, no?

**trials:** Riders earn points by "cleaning" (completing) a course of fifteen to forty sections that can feature stairs, ledges, benches, grinding rails, and narrow platforms called "skinnies." The trials can last two or three hours, depending on the difficulty and the riders' attention span.

**high jump and long jump:** Essentially, this is the same sport that athletes try without a unicycle: Riders hop over a bar or cross the ground, stick the dismount, and ride away to show control. The high-jump champ in 2008 cleared 3 feet 7 inches; the long-jump winner traveled 9 feet 4 inches.

Have a one-track mind? UNICON has all your options at www.unicon14.dk/gb/competitions.

> "[Polo is]
> like playing
> golf
> during an
> earthquake."
>
> —Sylvester Stallone

Pony polo, a four-versus-four game in which players on horse-back use a mallet to whack a ball toward a goal, claims a history of more than two millennia, as well as being *the* game of royalty, wealthy sportsmen, and those who have liked pretty ponies ever since their eighth birthday party. Originally called *pulu,* the Tibetan word for "ball," the game is said to have evolved from the military maneuvers of the ancient warriors of Central Asia, and eventually flourished among Persian tribes in the sixteenth and seventeenth centuries. Despite its tradition and ever-growing silhouette on col-lared shirts, "the sport of kings" on horses—or even horses on the snow or in an indoor arena, where the games are sometimes played nowadays—simply can't satisfy everyone. Some players feel the need to dispense with vehicles and power themselves in games of water polo. Still others prefer to kayak, cycle, or motor themselves around for the chukkas (seven-minute periods of play) the game requires.

## Elephant Polo

*"No elephant may lie down in front of the goal."*
—World Elephant Polo Association rule book

This sport, played exclusively in four countries—India and the three members of the World Elephant Polo Association: Thailand, Sri Lanka, and Nepal—presents all the challenges of pony polo, plus plenty of problems particular to playing perched upon pachyderms.

A game of elephant polo involves two teams of three elephants each, along with an elephant-mounted referee, on a bare field in each of two chukkas. Each "player" is actually a pair: The generally smaller mahout, the elephant handler, rides on the elephant's neck and steers with verbal commands and barefoot pressure; the larger, more fancily dressed player riding in the saddle wields the bamboo mallet that can be anywhere from 5 to 12 feet long. (It can be a long way down to the playing field, depending on the player's and the elephant's height.)

What's been true since the first elephants stepped onto the planet, let alone onto the manicured polo field, is that pachyderms don't maneuver quickly. Moreover, the sheer girth of animals often hides the ball once it's in play, and the competitors simply can't see it. (More helpful than just cheering "DE-FENSE! DE-FENSE!" as in other sports, fans actually call out the ball's whereabouts.) But one lithe and accidental trouncing by a half-ton (plus two riders) elephant can pack the ball into the playing field, which occasions a "restart."

Other rules? An elephant may not lie down in front of a goal,

---

### Yak Polo
### So what are you yakking about?

Not much of an equestrian? Not sure if you're up for partnering on a pachyderm? Looking to try a different family of beasts altogether? How about bovines? Hairy, horned central Asiatic ones?

Yak polo, a game that's supposed to "evoke the glories of the once-great Mongol empire," has served as a tourist attraction in Mongolia since 2006. While one might not think to describe a cousin of the cow as "versatile," yaks, which are not among the more trainable animals, are able to play on a variety of surfaces, including ice-covered rivers in the wintertime, when the temperature plummets to −22°F. Can that talent have actually improved wintertime tourism?

nor may one pick up the ball with its trunk. Oh, and there's one other trouble that plagues this version of polo: dung. Seven elephants, each of whom consumes some 175 pounds of food daily, will create 1,200 pounds of dung . . . at *some* point during the day of a competition.

Have an elephantine urge to join this "most exotic and exuberant" sport? Contact the World Elephant Polo Association: www.elephantpolo.com.

## Bicycle Polo

"If no one stays back, at, or near the goal, your opponent will fast break you to death until your lungs collapse and your long-term health is brought into question."
—U.S. Bicycle Polo Association "basic strategies"

"Welcome to the American Bicycle Polo Association of America," the Web site greets you. "What do you get when you combine the low-impact aerobic workout of cycling, the challenge of a racket sport, and the camaraderie of a team sport? Bicycle Polo!"

While players have a welcoming attitude and a penchant for answering their own riddles before providing time for others to guess, they also maintain strict rules and employ some remarkable strategies. For instance, "All players must play right-handed," and, according to the rules, may strike at a ball only "when the frame of the rider's bike has been parallel to the sideline for at least 21 feet (three bike lengths)." This ensures a "right of way" rule, which seeks to eliminate collisions, injuries, or anything else people look forward to in stock car races.

First played in the late nineteenth century by British troops in India, bike polo has seen the game go from its first international competition game in 1901 (an Irish win over the British), to the International Bicycle Polo Federation in 1996, to an annual world championship. Having established its popularity in Europe, bike polo now reaches as far east as Sri Lanka and Malaysia and as far west as the United States.

In each chukka, teams attempt to advance downfield in a staggered position, balancing the field so opponents cannot fast break. Skilled competitors can ride quickly, dribble the ball between their wheels, and even ride while juggling the ball on the mallet. Unskilled players wear nerdy knee guards, drop their mallets, slip off their bikes, and gain respect from other players by treating for ice cream after the game.

Tired of hearing, "Get me mint chocolate chip—a *double* dip!"? Stand in line at www.bicyclepolo.org.

## Canoe Polo

**"It's more white water than skim milk, more paddling than fraternity pledging."**
—Just a possible slogan for the 2010 Canoe Polo Championships

The horses that are truly suited for aquatic athletics are only a couple of inches long, eat brine shrimp, and look cute as can be with their tails wrapped around seaweed. Thus, the need arose for a "watered down"

version of pony polo, where players mount another trusty steed, the canoe.

In teams of five, players move in a canoe or kayak and use both paddles and hands to cross the "court." With the paddles, players propel themselves forward, dribble the ball, and even pass by scooping up the ball. Each player can possess the ball for five seconds max, so they also use their hands to pass or shoot into a netted goal suspended above the water. Because players attempt to capsize opponents and swing their paddles furiously, competitors wear life jackets with chest protectors, along with metal-grilled helmets.

It's uncertain whether the Bay City Scuba Club's hobbyhorse race at Port Phillip Bay, Victoria, Australia, has enough horse sense to win a place among the world's great underwater athletic competitions.

Since the time of the game's inception in the 1880s, when Scotsmen were seen playing polo in a river while straddling wooden barrels, the sport has reached over forty countries worldwide, twenty-three of which were represented at the Eighth World Canoe Polo Championships in 2008, a biennial event. While the Netherlands won the men's title and Great Britain took both the women's and men's under-twenty-one division, the United States failed to win a game in any of the three divisions. So much for our Eagle Scouts and their putative skills at damn near everything.

Have a friend with a pool and a few swimming noodles or ducky inner tubes? Get your feet wet at www.canoepolo.com.

## Segway Polo

*"Similar to real polo, but without the manure."*
—Segway polo enthusiast Alex Ko

Steve Wozniak's life has been quite the adventure. The Wizard of Woz co-invented the Apple computer, lost and regained his short-term memory after a plane crash, and dated comedian Kathy Griffin. Now, the caramel coating on this Apple icon's life is lending his name to the International Segway Human Transport Polo Tournament: the Woz Challenge Cup.

Segway polo, played on an electric-powered, two-wheeled vehicle programmed to balance itself, debuted during halftime of a Minnesota Vikings game in 2003. The following year, members of Bay Area Segway Enthusiasts began playing the game, and its popularity has soared ever since.

Teams of five play against one another at Segway's maximum speed, about 12.5 miles per hour. The rules feature "right of way"

violations, as it is illegal to cut off another player from an angle in order to avoid Segway collisions. (Unlike Wozniak, most players don't own *six more* of the $5,000 vehicles.)

The annual Woz Challenge Cup features teams from the United States, Germany, Spain, and New Zealand. In 2007, Wozniak's team, the Silicon Valley Aftershocks, defeated the New Zealand Pole Blacks to capture the championship. As if being selected to the National Inventors Hall of Fame wasn't enough for him?

Ready to spend five grand so you can be embarrassed by a sixtyish guy who's richer, better, and still richer than you? Visit www.segwayfest.com.

# eight

## Town Maul Meetings

We've all witnessed more than a few lame sports fights: soccer pretty-boys squaring up for a fisticuffs that pales in comparison to the ones taking place in the stands. A sixty-year-old, 5-foot 3-inch NBA referee stepping right between two towering, ready-to-brawl ballers and sending them to their respective corners for a time-out. A batter charging the pitcher's mound (and by "charging," this means approaching slowly and spewing threats) while both teams converge on the field for a brouhaha that's little more than a big ha-ha. (Fellas, if you mean to get serious, bring along a few bats.)

And just to prove how lame or blameless those "domesticated" sports appear, here are wilder sports that not only *allow* lawless behavior, but *require* it. Hardly confined to a manicured field or foul-line-bordered court, these sports are citywide scrums that involve minions: not merely varsity *and* junior varsity players, not merely one frat house against another, but literally thousands of people, as if a stadium of spectators suddenly took to the field. Whether fighting *with* food (*La Tomatina*), racing *for* food (cheese rolling), or battling in the land *of* food (Florence's *Calcio Storico*), these sprawling events take over town squares, cross miles of farmland, or wade naked into frigid streams. At these mob scenes, you won't even find a town sheriff trying to keep the peace—he's the one dressed like the Queen Mother or skidding down the hillside in pursuit of the coveted cheese.

Here's your free pass to the world of athletic free-for-alls.

**"Keep the ball out of the cemetery ... and players must not murder their opponents."**

—BBC

Imagine an NFL game. Now, round out that ball, lose the shoulder pads, and add a few hundred or even a thousand players to each team. Okay, now move the end zones 3 miles apart, and dam a river at the 50-yard line. Now you're ready for some Royal Shrovetide football.

Two games are played annually—one on Shrove Tuesday, the other on Ash Wednesday—in Ashbourne, Derbyshire, England. Shrovetide football is a citywide mob game that dispenses with million-dollar TV ads, along with any need for referees with their little yellow penalty flags to throw down at the first sign of excessive celebration.

The sport squares off two teams: those living north of the Henmore River are the up'ards; those living south are the down'ards.

Fortunately, those in the east and west have yet to realize that they've been left out of the ruckus.

While the game is called "football," there isn't much kicking involved. Instead, at 2:00 P.M. the game begins in the center of town. (Today that's the middle of a grocery store parking lot, which does make finding a parking space a bitch.) After a robust singing of "Auld Lang Syne" and "God Save the Queen," a visiting dignitary starts the game by "turning up" (tossing) the ball into the waiting crowd. Then all hell breaks loose as the ball is carried, thrown, or advanced in a scrumlike mass, an Ashburnian group hug, toward a goal that's many boisterous pubs and 3 long miles away.

If a goal is scored—a predetermined player honored with the chance to score must tap the ball three times against a symbolic stone marker—before 5:00 P.M., a new ball is put into play and the game continues until 10:00 P.M. If the first goal isn't scored until after 5:00 P.M., the game is called, and the pubs fill with sweaty win'ards and lose'ards who hang out until someone reminds the crowd that the kids at home still need to be fed.

Shrovetide football is said to have been played since the twelfth century, when the game "ball" was the head of an executed criminal. (It seems as if keep-away might have provided a better model for the game.) But the exact origins of the game were destroyed in 1891, when a fire ravaged the Royal Shrovetide Committee office. Modern games are played with a commemoratively painted leather ball filled with Portuguese cork (to prevent the ball from sinking during its likely submergence in the local river). Only twice in one hundred–plus years have the games been canceled: after the 1968 and 2001 outbreaks of foot-and-mouth disease.

Ashbourne invites anyone and everyone to take part in the "game." Try and fit in by learning the lyrics to the Shrovetide Anthem at the BBC's special tribute to the game: www.bbc.co.uk/derby/places/ashbourne_shrovetide_football.

## From the Actual Shrovetide Football Rule Book

Unnecessary violence frowned upon.
Ball can't be transported in a motor vehicle.
Ball must not be hidden in bags, rucksacks, coats, etc.
Keep the ball out of cemeteries, churchyards, and the
    Memorial Gardens.
Murder and manslaughter are barred.
No playing after 10:00 P.M.

**"No sucker punching, no kicking in the head, no convicted criminals allowed."**

—*Sports Illustrated*

Oh, and one more *recent* rule: Nobody "deemed too violent" from previous years' games may participate. (This successfully eliminated twenty players from the Green team in a single year.) Ideally, "too" and "violent" shouldn't be open to interpretation. But at Italy's *Calcio Storico Fiorentino,* one person's choke holds, head-butts, uppercuts, left jabs, and throwing of sand in opponents' eyes must be another person's idea of guys just being guys. Indeed, the cheering crowd expects and applauds such actions.

This five hundred-year-old blend of rugby, gladiatorial combat, and soccer (what most every other country, including Italy, calls "football") is played in Florence every summer by gents who, instead of perusing the galleries you visited once after taking an art-survey course, would rather get tattoos on their bald heads. In this four-team tournament, two twenty-seven-player squads face off at a time in a giant sand pit. For fifty minutes straight (time-outs are for naughty kids; substitutes are for maternity leaves), the Green, Red, Blue, and White teams, clad in sixteenth-century Italian garb, "play" to the sounds of rooting spectators and exploding team-colored smoke bombs.

First held in the 1500s by the Italian aristocracy (three popes even deigned to play), the spectacle saw its revival in 1930. Traditionally, a parade precedes the final game, which includes five hundred Florentines dressed in the Renaissance period's most chic ballooning pantaloons, flouncy sleeves, and angled berets. For a time, the procession allowed the players time to stop and pray at the church of Santa Maria Novella, until an ensuing brawl damaged a fifteenth-century fresco.

Not designed as a holy war, the object of the sport, technically speaking, is to score points, either by throwing the ball—a regular soccer ball—into the 50-meter-wide goal (one point) or by defending a

scoring attempt (one-half point). But for the majority of the fifty minutes, the teams, mostly composed of amateur boxers, stand in lines
bare-knuckle boxing. On occasion, someone does separate from the
punch-drunk chaos, typically a recruited rugby player who makes a run
to score as the pugilists look up, briefly curious about where that ball
came from, before continuing their best *Rocky* imitation. (They've got
the Italian accent down pretty well.)

Then the final bell sounds. . . . The winners receive a cow's worth
of steaks. Losers scuffle home from the bloody sandbox, past the Uffizi,
the Duomo, the David, the Pitti Palace . . . to pout.

**Kickboxer Mirko Cardelli continued to fight in a
tournament even after he'd busted both of his
hands. Among those now disqualified from future
play, he says: "The officials betrayed all of Florence
by changing the rules. I don't see why they have to
treat us like animals."**

**"Arrive at the top of the hill, check that your last will and testament is up-to-date, make sure that you won't need that pair of jeans ever again, and go!"**

—Official cheese rolling Web site

"As he flew to the bottom, his mother, my sister, and myself jumped the sideline to meet him. . . .We tumbled down to make sure he was okay as he lay unconscious."

And this, from the cousin of the *winner*.

Among the twenty competitors chasing a wheel of Double Gloucester that's speeding 70 miles per hour down the "majestic yet menacing" Cooper's Hill, twenty-year-old Christopher Anderson landed at the bottom first, winning the first heat in the 2008 cheese-rolling competition in Gloucester, England. His prize, besides the neck brace and the free stretcher ride "to hospital": the cheese. (Actual retail value, about $136.)

Injuries are commonplace for the two hundred–year-old tradition that "could have evolved from early fertility rites and hopes of a successful harvest" or as a way "to safeguard the 'Commoners Rights' of the inhabitants of the hill." Yeah, or it could have been a terrible misunderstanding or a translation error or just someone mistaking a dropped wheel of cheese for something of genuine national import, such as a limited-edition model of a *Doctor Who* time-traveling police box.

Groups of competitors sit in line at the hill's crest for each of the five downhill races (three men's, two women's), which alternate with uphill races, including two for children. The master of ceremonies—generally, a local dairy farmer who loses office only through retirement or, more commonly, death—is helped up the slope by an invited guest. Each race begins with that timeless jingle, "One to be ready, two to be steady, three to prepare, four to be off!" at which point the MC flings the hapless cheese down the grassy slope. Minutes later, at the

foot of the hill, rugby players tackle any skidding competitors before anyone topples the awaiting fence or cheering spectators.

The participants' greatest concern is the hill's steepness: "I'm sure it's vertical; if you tilt your head slightly and sort of squint out of your left eye, you can just about see a slight curve to it—just," described one participant. Indeed, the hill's grade is, at points, one-in-one as the Brits say—that is, for each horizontal foot, the hill rises one vertical foot. At points, the slope drops at a 70-degree angle. (Got the picture? Twenty more degrees would be jumping off a cliff.)

The greatest concern to the over 2,500 spectators is the cheese itself. The 7- or 8-pound wheel careening crazily down the hill is heavy and fast enough to be classified as a missile by local standards.

Fondue-fork fencing just isn't enough of a sport for you? Try www.cheese-rolling.co.uk.

# Rolling Through the Years

Mix a ridiculously dangerous sport with two hundred years of English-men who wash down their cheese with scrumpy (that's English cider—alcoholic content generally 7.5 percent), and you've got a fairly colorful serving of history. Here are some highlights:

**1800s:** Cooper's Hill Wake, originally a religious festival, expands its celebration to include cheese-rolling races, as well as "grinning through a horse's collar for a cake," "bobbing for penny loaves smeared in treacle" (thick syrup), and shin kicking.

**1941–1954:** Food rationing requires the race to use wooden wheels of cheese with a token bit of real cheese secured in the center.

**1978:** Stephen Gyde grabs the first of the twenty-one cheeses he'll win over the next fourteen years. He remains the only man to win all three men's races twice, in 1980 and 1991.

**1982:** Lightning strikes eight people during the competition, including four children. Races resume after the weather clears.

**1983:** Wearing nothing but a T-shirt and jockstrap, "Digger" Gardner wins one cheese and one second place, admitting that the outfit "did wonders for streamlining."

**1988:** Local cheesemaker Diana Smart remains the only person in Gloucestershire to make the double wheels by hand, and provides the prize for all races.

**1990:** The races put twenty-two competitors and spectators into ambulances, including a fifty-nine-year-old grandmother, a spectator who was undercut by a cheese.

**1997:** Event injuries reach a new high of thirty-seven people, including seven onlookers. One winner breaks his left arm; having broken his right arm on the hill years earlier, he earns a double fracture for his Double Gloucester.

**1998:** Police ban the event: The injured, thirty-seven, now outnumber the population of Cooper's Hill, thirty-six.

**1999:** Committee members improve safety precautions and the cheese rolls once again.

## "Tomatoes must be crushed before throwing."

—www.spanish-fiestas.com

The sport of *La Tomatina* obeys many laws of science:

There's physics: Spherical projectiles move through space with a predictable diminishing velocity as they encounter resistance, inertia, and correlation bounce. Chaos theory also comes into play.

Elements of biology are there, too: Organisms of the species *Homo sapiens* exhibit survival-of-the-fittest skills in a complex micro-ecosystem.

The central theme of *La Tomatina* is botanical, centered on *Lycopersicon lycopersicum,* a herbaceous, usually sprawling plant in the Solanaceae family (common name, tomato).

There's meteorology: how to forecast a gross front moving in, with a good chance of ketchup showers.

But contrary to all this evidence, *La Tomatina,* an annual, citywide tomato riot, remains an inexact science. One would think that after sixty-three—or is it sixty-four?—years, the residents of Buñol, Valencia, Spain, would have their facts straight. Some say *La Tomatina* uses 150,000 tomatoes. Other claim the number is over one million. Various sources declare that the weight of the flying fruit totals 90,000 pounds, 224,000 pounds, or maybe 280,000 pounds (that's 140 tons).

Historians, let alone tomato hurlers, don't even know how this insanity began, although the holiday was banned at one point "for having no religious significance." Some say the tradition began when diners got out of hand at a local restaurant. Others think tomatoes were used to appease a youngster who had turned violent after trying to join a parade of *Gigantes y Cabezudos* (giant figures with big heads)

and unintentionally knocked one over. Another version tells the story of locals using the fruit to attack an unpopular city councilman at a town festival.

There is consensus on one thing: The world's largest food fight results in a bowl of salsa the size of a town square with twenty thousand—or is it fifty thousand?—humans dipping in like tortilla chips.

Held on the last Wednesday in August as part of a festival to honor Buñol's patron saint, the battle begins when a courageous participant ascends a 20-foot greased wooden pole to retrieve a coveted ham. (Once again, asking "why?" only yields further mystery and groans from those who keep kosher.) The blasts of water cannons then signal the official start of the fight, during which participants must squish the tomatoes for safety precautions. Goggles are also highly recommended, in addition to a standard uniform of a T-shirt and shorts destined for the garbage. After an hour, during which time everything turns shades of pink and red, cannons are fired again to signal the end of the war. Fire trucks then hose down the town and flush the pulp away. Marvelously, the tomatoes (their pH ranges from 3.9 to 4.9, with citric acid being the most abundant component) actually acid-wash the streets clean.

Even science couldn't engineer an ending that perfect.

Seeing red already? Look into www.latomatina.org.

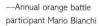

**"It's not violent, but it is a way to release your own inner violence."**

—Annual orange battle participant Mario Bianchi

Unlike that of *La Tomatina,* the ammunition at Italy's *Carnevale di Ivrea*'s orange battle doesn't get squished before being hurled in the streets. It may, however, become smushed after colliding with the helmets that keep faces from leaking their own natural juices.

Held since the nineteenth century, the orange battle represents a rebellion against feudal lords waged in 1194. Or, as another story goes, commoners incited a riot when a local woman presented the head of the marquis from her balcony; the cruel leader had attempted to deflower her on the eve of her wedding. Today, in the name of democracy, monogamy, or vitamin C, three thousand people divided into nine teams (they represent the rebellious commoners) bombard six-person horse-drawn carriages of "castle defenders" (they represent the guards of the aristocracy)

with a barrage of one million oranges.

Judges, including the castle defenders themselves, give awards to the top-performing teams, each stationed at a particular "battleground." Fortunately for some squads, awards aren't based on their nicknames. Teams such as Death and the Mercenaries try to turn the castle defenders to pulp, while the Chessmen disprove the notion that they're merely pawns.

# Rioja's Wine Battle

## (Batalla del Vino)

> "Mass starts, and after this, the battle."
>
> —City of Haro Tourist Board

In this juiced-up battle, the grapes have already been squished and fermented, so participants need only wineskins, plastic jugs, trash cans, water guns, or crop sprayers to spill, spritz, and splash the other nine thousand revelers at the

*Batalla del Vino* or "Wine Battle," in Haro, part of Spain's Rioja region.

Held at the end of June every year, the alcoholic affray symbolizes a past dispute over the ownership of the Bilibios Mounts with a neighboring village. After the town holds a giant mass, there is a procession to the hills, and between 8,000 and 10,000 gallons of wine are poured, allaying every average diner's bafflement: "Who needs a sommelier? Just *plonk* it down here!"

While participants arrive dressed in all white—the crowd looks as if it's auditioning for a cream cheese commercial—they leave with shirts and skin stained lavender. There haven't been this many purple lunatics since the big Tinky Winky versus Barney the Dinosaur match at Caesar's Palace.

## "Tattoos bring everyone bad luck."

—World Events Guide

Another of Japan's naked festivals, the *hadaka* at Saidaiji Temple in Okamaya, is, once again, all about luck. Except, instead of sharing good fortune, for one night every February, ten thousand tattoo-less men gather at the Buddhist temple to fight for it: one of two sacred sticks (*shingi*) said to guarantee luck for the possessor. (The last sticks on record as creating such fanaticism were ones Ringo Starr threw into a mob of teenage girls.)

Participants change in a dressing tent, where "volunteers" spend hours giving wedgies to all the men. The loincloth (*fundoshi*) is so tightly secured around the waist and between the buttocks that there's little chance of donning the requisite socks (*tabi*) if you'd forgotten them.

The five hundred–year-old tradition is said to date back to

times when priests, after completing ascetic training at the temple, received paper amulets (*Go-o*) as a token of their accomplishment. Later, at festivals held on the temple grounds, priests began distributing the symbolic talismans to worshipers. Annually, as the crowds grew larger and the amulets more lucky, apparently, the crowds became more and more aggressive in trying to obtain the papers. Over the years, folks realized that a pair of sticks was less likely to tear than paper.

Today, wrestling for the *shingi* is preceded by a night of festivities—a mob of boys wrestle for rice cakes (*mochi*, which are never apple cinnamon or Cheddar cheese), fireworks explode (probably to a patriotic sound track featuring the Japanese equivalent of Bruce Springsteen), and competitors ritually cleanse themselves in the nearby Yoshi River, despite the February temperature, which hovers around freezing. Yes, a few cups of warm sake helps.

Participants then run laps around the temple to visit the different Buddhist deities before entering the main room to jockey for the best positions. At midnight, the lights go off and the *shingi* are tossed

into the crowd, where, for exactly one hour, the horde jostles for the holy sticks, all the while chanting the traditional, *"Wasshoi! Wasshoi! Wasshoi!"*—the Japanese equivalent of "Heave ho!" Some duck under people's legs. Some climb over others' heads. Some men work together in teams; it's easy to imagine them drawing up the X's and O's of their strategy. (Try not to imagine John Madden in a loincloth.) Some offer bribes to fellow competitors: "Fifty-five hundred yen? Sure, that'll get me a kid's pass to Tokyo Disneyland, but . . . " Many end up bruised or bloodied.

At the end of the melee, any man who managed to thrust a *shingi* into a wooden box full of rice (*masu*) is said to be the luckiest in Japan. And the luck spreads! A pregnant woman who wraps herself in a festival-worn *fundoshi* will give birth to a healthy child. A field will yield a bountiful harvest if the dirt tracked into the temple is sprinkled there. And, despite the countless germs that an hour's worth of bumping, wrestling, and "ritual cleansing" in a frigid river provides, ten thousand participants are guaranteed a year without a cold.

# photo credits

Most grateful acknowledgment is extended to the many photographers who generously contributed their works:

Barefooting: Michael Digby
BASE Jumping: Prakash Gopalakrishnan; Skysurfing: Joe Jennings; Swooping: Christo Boshoff
Bavarian Finger Wrestling: Jay Morthland; Toe Wrestling: Adrian Hon
Bog Snorkeling: (snorkeling) Andrew Cook; (cycling) Sheelagh Tompkins
Bossaball: Mohammad Faleh Al-Saleh
Broomball: (close-up) James M. Turley; (others) Robert Green
Caber Toss (and other timber sports): (caber) John Haslam; (others) Christine Estacio
*Calcio Storico*: Tommaso Baldovino
Cheese Rolling: Jean Jefferies
Chess Boxing: Yves Sucksdorff © WCBO
Croquet: (extreme) Lakewood Croquet Club; (mondo) Kathleen Miller, LMP, LMT
Cyclocross: Joe Sales
The Devil's Jump: Carlos González Ximénez
Extreme Cold-Water Swimming: (man diving) courtesy Morrissey & Co.; (man in water)
    Maxim Tupikov
Extreme Ironing: (cave) Ben Stevens; (underwater) Andrew Newton
Fierjleppen: (image of split-legged jumper) Lianne van der Wijk; (graph and all other
    photos)Polsstokbond Holland
Hurling: (egg) Stephen Preston; (haggis) Monkey Business Images; (human cannonball)
    Andy Hornby; (fruitcake) Christina Lutze
Ice Race: (automobile) Eric Bégin; (motorcycle) Keetra Baker
Irish Road Bowling: Paul McMann
Joggling: Vincent Nail
Kabaddi: Taginder Singh Saini
Kiiking: courtesy of www.kiiking.ee
Land and Ice Sailing: (ice) Peter Dutton; (land) Blokart International Archive
Mower Racing: David Byrne
Mudslinging: David M. Weber
Naked Men Festival (*Hadaka Matsuri*): Yoshio Wada
Octopush: Brian Cripe; cover photo by Grégory Piazzola

Orange Battle (*Carnevale di Ivrea*): Robero Pagini (www.alookthroughlens.com)

Outhouse Racing: (Brown Streak; Crap Shoot) Brian Rossow (Two Harbors, Minnesota, Winter Frolic); (Lady Justice; Potty; Startling Line) Dean Franklin

Polos: (elephant) Linda Rodgers; (canoe) Choo Yut Shing; (Segway) Leslie Chicoine; (hobbyhorse) Andrew Newton

Retro Cycling: (man with hat) Clayton Hackett; (other) MJR

Retro Running: (running) MJR; (race) Lucy Andrews; (sign) Matthew Klein

Rock, Paper, Scissors: posters courtesy of www.worldrps.com; photo by Conway Yen

Sauna: Maiju Saari

Sepak Takraw: Shutterstock

Shin Kicking: Betty Stocker

Shovel Racing: John Strader

Shrovetide Football: Wayne Harrison

Skijøring: (horse) Shannon Maguire; (dog) Jamie Myers

Skimboarding and Sandboarding: (skim) Blazej Maksym; (skim shots of Venezuela) courtesy of Eduardo Espinoza; (sand) Shutterstock

Soccers: (swamp): Swamp Soccer U.K. Ltd.; (snow) Jason Teale

Speedball: courtesy of Dr. Ahmed Lofty, World Speedball Federation

Speed Cubing: David Belleville

Spitting: (sunflower) Tory Tish; (watermelon): Carri Heisler; (kudu) Hans Hemmes

Splash Diving: Kultos Entertainment/Ch Pollok

Sport Stacking: courtesy of WSSA

Stone Skipping: (Russ Byers) Nate Beggs; (skipping stones and dog) courtesy of Russ Byers

Street Luge: Sherman Stibbens

Tiller Racing: (Billy Robertson) Billy Dailey; (Lauri Waller) Hal Miller

Tomato Battle (*La Tomatina*): David W. Dellinger; (crowd with tomatoes) Aaron C. Smith

Tower Jumping: Julius Hrivnac

Underwater Football: (basketball flood) Tony L. Jones; (football flood) David H. Tribby

Unicycle Sports: Cedric Blanc (www.cedric-blanc.com)

Wife-Carrying Race: courtesy Sunday River

Wine Battle (*Batalla del Vino*): courtesy of the City of Haro Tourist Board

*Yukigassen*: photos by Yuji Shishikura and posters courtesy of Showa-Shinzan International Yukigassen Committee

**Other images:**

naked tug-o-war (xv): courtesy www.burningman.com and photographer Sharon Fila

wheelbarrow race (xi): Philip Currie

foot with hash marks (xiii); man racing in grocery cart (viii); jumping on bed (220); and racing store coin-op horse (x) Timothy Wheaton

Town Crier Competition (ix): Cory Blundon

vintage photos (ii, 18, 224): George Grantham Bain Collection (Library of Congress)

# list of sports